Writing @ 7200 Feet

A Beginner's Guide to College Composition and Rhetoric

Second Edition

Shelby Hutson

Nancy Small

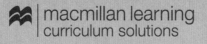

macmillan learning
curriculum solutions

Macmillan Learning Curriculum Solutions
14903 Pilot Drive
Plymouth, MI 48170
www.macmillanlearning.com

SmallN 9297-3 F18

macmillan learning
curriculum solutions

Sustainability
Hayden-McNeil's standard paper stock uses a minimum of 30% post-
consumer waste. We offer higher % options by request, including a 100%
recycled stock. Additionally, Hayden-McNeil Custom Digital provides authors
with the opportunity to convert print products to a digital format. Hayden-
McNeil is part of a larger sustainability initiative through Macmillan Learning.
Visit http://sustainability.macmillan.com to learn more.

bedford/st. martin's • hayden-mcneil
w.h. freeman • worth publishers

Writing @ 7200 Feet

A Beginner's Guide to College Composition and Rhetoric
Second Edition

Table of Contents

Section One: Introduction to College-Level Writing 29

Chapter One: What Is "Academic" Writing? 31

Chapter Two: Navigating Genres 45

Questions to Ask About Your Own Projects 57

Section Two: Reading and Writing as
Integrated Processes 59

Chapter Three: Reading Processes 61

Chapter Four: A Writer's Choices:
An Overview of the Writing Process 71

This book is dedicated to the University of Wyoming writing community, of which you are now a member.

Welcome. We're glad you're here.

Letter from the Editors

Dear Readers (and Writers):

Welcome to English 1010 and to the University of Wyoming! This book has been specially designed for our program. We hope it helps you understand that academic writing is fueled by interest and passion, and is structured by rhetorical moments and situations. Furthermore, we hope this book helps you become more confident academic and lifelong writers.

You'll notice this second edition of *Writing @ 7200 Feet* has six sections, each containing content hand picked to address the needs of beginning academic writers. The Introduction situates writing within our university context. It includes information about UW, communication (COM) requirements, and programs or services related to writing. It also includes general class policies and details on the portfolio system we use. Our class is taught in terms of "genres" or types of writing, so Section 1 materials provide more information about that approach. Reading and writing are interwoven activities—practicing and growing your skills in one usually means practicing and growing your skills in the other. Therefore, Section 2 emphasizes both processes. Building off the foundations laid in the initial readings, Sections 3, 4, and 5 delve into more detail on different aspects of the writing process, including how to build an argument, how to use sources, and how to get the most from peer review. Although our class focuses on academic writing in different genres, the advice in this book applies to all writers, at all levels, and in all disciplines.

What else do you need to be successful in English 1010? The answer is more details and coaching on your specific project assignments, homework, and in-class activities. In class, your instructor will introduce you to the online space where such information will be located. Make sure to get familiar with that space and study the materials carefully. Feel free to browse—don't wait for your instructor to point out every detail! As the semester commences, you'll also have access to your instructor through office hours and through project-related conferences. Take advantage of these opportunities. Getting to know your instructor and receiving individual feedback or coaching can lead to much greater learning in any course.

We owe a big debt of gratitude to people who have made UW's writing program the strong intellectual community that it is today. Kelly Kinney and Joyce Stewart have provided generous expertise as previous leaders of our writing programs. April Heaney, David Bray, Allison Gernant, Peter Parolin, Rick Fisher, Jason Kirkmeyer, and Matt Drollette have been and continue to be important mentors. The Graduate Assistants who teach so many of our English 1010 classes are smart, engaged, and active contributors to making the course a success. And the 2017–2018 Writing Programs Committee—including Brianna Casey, James Creel, Michael Knievel, and Kenneth Thompson—has provided useful advice on how we can continually improve. Without this network of colleagues, friendships, and conversations, our work would not be possible. Finally, a special shout-out to our cover photographer, Elizabeth Traver, as well as to the photographers who provided our section divider shots, Zach Hutson and Ankita Sawant. We appreciate that your work brings the beauty of Wyoming into the pages of this book.

We're glad you are here, reading and writing students, and we wish you the best possible semester, as well as a bright future in being part of academic and community conversations.

Shelby Hutson
Assistant Director of Writing Programs
MA Program in English

Nancy Small
Director of Writing Programs
Assistant Professor of English

Introduction

To help you understand the contexts and goals for English 1010, this section begins with our broadest guiding text: the University of Wyoming's Mission Statement. From there, we narrow down to the mission of the first-year writing program and then to the specific course description and learning outcomes for English 1010. As you work through this course and start thinking about continuing to grow your communication skills, check out the information in this section on our COM2 and COM3 courses, on our Professional Writing Minor, and on our undergraduate journal, *Inside English 1010*. UW's Writing Center is an excellent resource for writers at all levels, so more details on it are here, too. Finally, you'll find course policies and a FAQ about portfolio grading in the following pages. As you read through those, you should also give your class syllabus—provided the first meeting and found online—another careful review.

UW Mission Statement

The University of Wyoming aspires to be one of the nation's finest public land-grant research universities. We serve as a statewide resource for accessible and affordable higher education of the highest quality; rigorous scholarship; technology transfer; economic and community development; and responsible stewardship of our cultural, historical, and natural resources.

In the exercise of our primary mission to promote learning, we seek to provide academic and co-curricular opportunities that will:

- Expose students to the frontiers of scholarship and creative activity and the complexities of an interdependent world;

- Ensure individual interactions among students, faculty, and staff;

- Nurture an environment that values and manifests diversity, free expression, academic freedom, personal integrity, and mutual respect; and

- Promote opportunities for personal growth, physical health, athletic competition, and leadership development for all members of the university community.

As Wyoming's only university, we are committed to outreach and service that extends our human talent and technological capacity to serve the people in our communities, our state, the nation, and the world.

First-Year Writing Program Mission Statement

Committed to providing highly motivated students an outstanding education grounded in a spirit of public intellectualism, the First-Year Writing Program is a central component of the University of Wyoming English Department. Our mission is to foster the academic and civic literacies essential for success at the university and beyond. To this end, we offer students a rigorous course that meets the COM1 general education requirement, and provide faculty and graduate assistants an intensive mentoring program that supports state-of-the-art instruction.

The course central to this commitment is English 1010: College Composition and Rhetoric, which asks students to communicate in different genres for a range of audiences, engage in intensive revision, and practice critical thinking through researched argumentation. Laying a general foundation for writing at the University of Wyoming, the course maintains a significant emphasis on scholarly research, including how to formulate appropriate research questions; how to find, evaluate, and integrate a range of credible sources; and how to add one's perspectives to ongoing scholarly and civic conversations. Since the fall of 2016, the course also integrates exciting multimodal genres that satisfy University Studies Program objectives to support students' understanding of and facility with digital literacies.

By focusing on salient issues important in the civic and academic spheres, English 1010 is also in keeping with one of the UW's most time-honored traditions: that is, to nurture in students "responsible stewardship of our cultural, historical, and natural resources."

English Department USP COM Overview

English COM1: English 1010

English 1010 is the primary COM1 course satisfying UW's University Studies Program (USP) learning outcomes. It is designed to help students meet a wide range of writing, reading, and oral communication competencies, listed below. Students must complete this COM1 course in order to enroll in a COM2.

Course Description and Learning Outcomes

ENGL 1010 is designed to help first-year students like you become stronger writers, speakers, and critical thinkers, and it features assignments that allow you to explore issues that matter in the university community and the broader civic sphere. The course requires you to engage in different genres for a range of audiences, emphasizes revision, and gives you practice in critical thinking and researched writing. Much of your coursework in ENGL 1010 will emphasize how and why writing conventions differ according to their rhetorical situations. The course's emphasis on civic discourse is in keeping with one of the University of Wyoming's central missions: to help reinforce in students a sense of responsibility for adding their voices to important public conversations.

ENGL 1010 satisfies the COM1 University Studies Program general education requirement. By the end of the term, students who successfully complete the course will demonstrate the ability to:

1. Develop and communicate ideas in writing using appropriate technologies.

2. Find, evaluate, analyze, synthesize, and appropriately document information from a variety of sources in order to support a persuasive argument.

3. Recognize the importance of purpose, audience, and style as components of effective communication.

4. Strategically use a range of critical reading approaches to read and respond to college-level texts.

5. Make effective use of multiple drafts, revision, computer technology, peer and instructor comments, and collaboration in the achievement of a final work of communication.

6. Observe the accepted conventions of spelling, grammar, structure, and punctuation for Standard English.

7. Recognize similarities and differences in purposes and strategies of written, oral, and digital communication.

COM2 and COM3 Offerings

The English department offers a wide range of useful COM2 and COM3 courses. Check our website for more details, including course descriptions.

Current COM2 courses include
*   English 2005: Writing in Technology and Sciences

*   English 2015: Composition and Rhetoric II

*   English 2020: Literature, Media, and Culture
    These sections often have interesting themes like cartoons, vampires, or zombies.

*   English 2025: Introduction to English Studies
    This class is only for English majors and for those considering English as a major.

*   English 2035: Writing for Public Forums

Current COM3 courses include
*   English 3020: Culture, Communication, and the Workplace

*   English 4000: 21st Century Issues in Professional Writing

*   English 4010: Technical Writing in the Professions

*   English 4025: Writing for the Web

*   English 4075: Writing for Non-Profits

*   English 4999: Senior Seminar for English Majors

If you have questions about which COM courses are more appropriate for your major and interests, check with your academic advisor or contact the English department at 307-766-6452.

The Professional Writing Minor and the Literary Studies Minor

As you consider what minor (or minors) will complement your major course of study, ponder the English Department's options. The **Professional Writing Minor** works well with most any major—we routinely have professional writing minors who major in business, in the sciences, in the social sciences, and in the humanities. Writing and communication is an essential part of almost any career path and is central to professional success. Our minor is designed to help you think critically about writing *now* while preparing for what's to come *after* you graduate from UW.

The Professional Writing Minor can help you fulfill your COM2 and COM3 requirements while exposing you to writing and communication in a wide range of contexts and environments. Choose from courses such as Writing for the Web, Writing in Technology and the Sciences, Writing for Public Forums, Writing for Non-Profits, Editing for Publications, Magazine Writing, and Technical Writing in the Professions. The Professional Writing Minor offers opportunities to write, communicate, and learn valuable skills and approaches across print and digital media platforms that you will use in your professional and civic lives.

Do you love to read literature? Then the department also offers a **Minor in Literary Studies**. It invites you to take a variety of courses in fiction, non-fiction, poetry, and specialized courses focuses on particular authors. The Minor in Literary Studies will grow your perspectives on the world and your critical thinking strategies, even as it continues to build your communication skills.

To find out more about either minor, visit our web page (www.uwyo.edu/english/) and use the left-hand navigation menu to find undergraduate resources and links to the minor. You're also welcome to contact the department at 307-766-6452.

About the UW Writing Center

The Writing Center offers you the opportunity to conference with an experienced writer who genuinely wants to listen to and discuss your writing. The consultant's goal is to suggest focused writing and revising strategies that can help you not only improve your current paper but also transfer skills to other writing projects as well.

The Writing Center works with writers and instructors across UW, both on- and off-campus, and they provide free assistance in writing to UW students, faculty, and staff in all departments and at all levels.

What Kinds of Writing Does the Writing Center Help With?

The Writing Center offers free one-on-one, 30-minute conferences or group conferences. Writers may come in at any time in the writing process (brainstorming, development, rough draft, revisions, etc.). Writing Center consultants can help with all kinds of writing tasks, such as:

- research papers
- class papers
- résumés
- citation/documentation
- graduate theses
- lab reports
- poetry
- essay examinations
- job applications
- graduate school applications
- grants

What Happens During a Typical Writing Center Conference?

When you arrive for your conference, a member of the Writing Center will greet you and ask you a few questions about your writing project. If it is course-related, you will be asked at the beginning or the end of your conference to identify the course and the instructor. It saves time if you have that information readily available.

The best conferences are those initiated by writers who come with a clear sense of purpose or specific questions:

- Some students ask the Writing Center to help them understand an assignment and brainstorm ideas.

- Other students come with a rough draft and questions regarding organization and clarity.

- Some students come with drafts or graded essays on which the instructor has written specific comments regarding their writing.

Since the Writing Center wants you to better understand your purpose, audience, and focus and to become a more self-sufficient writer, a consultant will not take your paper and write on it or correct it. Instead, through questions and discussion, you will be encouraged to make your own informed decisions about your writing.

How Can You Make an Appointment?

The Writing Center is often available to accommodate drop-ins; however, during their busy weeks (during midterms, before and after breaks, and the weeks prior to finals) it's best to make an appointment. You can make appointments for in-person or online writing consultations by visiting the Writing Center web page and creating an account with their scheduling application. Writers can sign up for thirty-minute or sixty-minute appointments up to four times per week, as needed. If you have trouble creating an account or scheduling an appointment, you can call the Writing Center at 307-766-5250 or you can visit them in Coe Library 302. The Writing Center is generally open Monday–Friday, 9:00am–7:00pm. You can find out more information regarding Writing Center workshops, resources, events, etc. by visiting www.uwyo.edu/ctl/writing-center/.

One Last Question: Will the Writing Center Proofread Your Paper?

The Writing Center is a good resource for learning how to improve the grammar and mechanics of your writing, but it is not an editing service. Writing Center faculty will not edit or proofread your paper. They will, instead, read some or all of the paper with you to identify recurring errors and help you learn to recognize and correct them. Additionally, they cannot guarantee that a conference will improve the grade on the writing you discuss, since grades may reflect many factors that have not been discussed during a conference.

An Additional Option for Evening Help in ENGL 1010

ENGL 1010 tutoring is also available in the evenings through the STEP Tutor Center, located in Coe Library. Writing-Center-trained tutors can help with any stage in the writing process (brainstorming, development, rough draft, revisions, etc.). Sessions are drop in (no appointments) and are 30 minutes in length. Students who seek academic help for this class tend to perform 15–20% better than students who do not. The STEP Tutor Schedule (www.uwyo.edu/studentaff/step/) contains more information about this great resource.

Call for Papers: Inside English 1010

Inside English 1010 is a publication of the Writing Programs in the Department of English at the University of Wyoming. The journal's mission is to showcase how English 1010 students have met the challenge of tackling assignments. Students should think of the essays in the journal not as patterns to strictly imitate but as samples and examples of successful rhetorical choices other writers have made. With your English 1010 instructor and classmates, you can read several or all of the essays and analyze differences and similarities among them.

Current English 1010 students—here's why you should submit your work for review and potential publication:

- Getting published looks great on a résumé: it's an accomplishment that few undergraduates achieve.

- Getting published feels great: you'll feel proud of your work.

- You'll learn about the process of publication.

- You'll help future students and instructors see how differently students can successfully tackle English 1010 assignments.

- You'll get to brag that you are a published author!

Prior to leaving town after finals week, send your very best final drafts of English 1010 essays to:

insideenglish1010@gmail.com

Submitted work will be reviewed by a panel of English 1010 instructors and considered for publication in next year's edition of *Inside English 1010*.

- Remember to attach the essay as a Word .doc or .docx file ONLY (not .odt, .PDF, etc.).

- Make sure your Works Cited is included as part of the file. Do not send it as a separate file.

- To give yourself the best chance to be published, don't send work before you've completed final revisions during the last two weeks of classes.

Good luck and happy writing!

Classroom Policies for English 1010

ENGL 1010: College Composition and Rhetoric

Required Materials
Materials for English 1010 are located in two places:

- This book
- The online course space

You will receive information about the online course space during the first class meeting. Bookmark it and check it often. Materials related to course projects, homework, and other activities will be located in this space. Please note that accessing this space is mandatory. Forgetting to check it may impact your grade.

Course Policies
Course Structure
On many days, the class will be conducted in seminar format, which means you will engage in discussions about reading, writing, and speaking assignments and examine the rhetorical strategies used to persuade audiences. As a class, we will raise questions, pose problems, interpret readings, challenge one another's ideas, and develop strategies for successfully completing assignments. There will also be many class sessions in which we perform small group activities, including peer review, conferencing, drafting, and editing. Although there will be mini-lectures on a variety of writing-related topics, we will spend the majority of class time engaging in collaborative discussions and activities.

Drafting Requirements, Due Dates, and Deadline Extensions
You must turn in full drafts of assignments and perform your oral presentations on the days they are due. *Failure to meet word count requirements or deadlines can result in failure of the assignment and/or course.* Please note that students may not submit a final portfolio that contains a draft that the instructor has not examined in an earlier state. If you anticipate needing a deadline extension for a draft, you may request one *at least one week in advance of the due date.* Instructors have the right to deny deadline extensions and/or implement appropriate penalties when you turn in late work. Important note: *Instructors will not give deadline extensions for midterm and final portfolios.*

Classroom Participation

You should come to every class, on time, fully prepared. You are expected to fulfill all homework, presentation, and reading requirements. Invest yourself in presentations, readings, and discussions—doing so will pay off in enhancing your writing abilities. Because one of the objectives of ENGL 1010 is to make you comfortable engaging in different forms of public discourse—both written and oral—you should make an effort to add your voice to discussions during class. Failing to participate regularly will negatively impact your course grade.

Workshop, Peer Critique, and Sharing Your Work

When you meet in groups to give and receive peer feedback, it is your responsibility to have a complete draft and to bring enough copies for everyone in your group. Failing to do so usually results in being marked absent. Sharing your writing is perhaps the single most important activity of this course. Take peer critique seriously and work hard to establish the kind of climate that will make it successful. Your instructor may also request drafts to share with the entire class or with other instructors of ENGL 1010. You certainly may decline such requests. Note, though, that you can trust that all work you share in and outside the classroom will be treated with respect.

Technology Requirements

English 1010 requires the following:

- Frequent access to the internet for online materials,

- Frequent access to uwyo.edu email in case of class announcements and/or to communicate with your instructor,

- Occasional access to a printer (color is sometimes preferred but not required).

Project instructions, homework details, and other course information will be posted online. Your instructor will show you how to access that online space the first day of class. Forgetting to check or locate materials there may result in a grade deduction.

Your instructor can only communicate with you via email using your uwyo.edu address or through your WyoCourse "Inbox." Please do not send email from other accounts. Check your email daily to make sure you don't miss any news from your instructor. You are welcome to send questions via uwyo.edu to your instructor and can expect a response within 24 hours on weekdays and within 48 hours if a weekend is included.

Finally, you need consistent access to a working computer and printer for this course. UW students have limited computer and printing privileges in campus labs. Nevertheless, whether you use your private computer and printer or public ones, you alone are responsible for saving and backing up all of your written work and printing it out in time to meet deadlines: if you fail to do so, you risk losing points in the course.

Plagiarism and UW's Academic Honesty Code

All members of the university community have a responsibility to be honest and the right to expect honesty from others. Instructors and students should report suspected violations of standards of academic honesty to the instructor, program director, department head, or dean. In keeping with *UW's Honesty Code*, ENGL 1010 prohibits acts of *plagiarism*. For the purpose of this course plagiarism is defined as presenting the writing or ideas of others as one's own without appropriate attribution and citation. Plagiarism ranges from submitting a paper written by someone else, to copying partial paragraphs or sentences without proper attribution, to duplicating sentence structures, ideas, or information from any source without proper attribution.

Plagiarism includes

- quoting, paraphrasing, or summarizing without acknowledgment, even a few phrases;
- failing to acknowledge the source of a major idea or principle central to one's work;
- relying on another person's data, evidence, or critical method without credit;
- submitting another person's work as one's own, including assignment drafts, classroom activities, and homework; and
- borrowing ideas from unacknowledged sources, including both print and digital sources.

If you are unsure how or when to cite sources, do not hesitate to ask for help. Please note, however, that it is every student's responsibility to follow these policies, and failure to do so can range from failing an assignment, or failing the course, to academic probation, suspension, or even expulsion.

Class Conduct

According to the *Student Code of Conduct* (www.uwyo.edu/dos/conduct/), "Students have the responsibility to respect the instructor's freedom to teach and the right of other students to learn. Students have the responsibility to maintain reasonable standards of conduct established by the instructor for each class." Of course, it is vital that all students contribute to class discussion, but your contributions should be thoughtful, relevant, and above all, respectful of your peers and instructor. Unnecessary talking, texting, sleeping, or reading unrelated material during class is disruptive and will not be tolerated. Students who fail to follow class conduct guidelines will be penalized and in severe causes, according to university policy, may be expelled from the course.

Grade Appeal Policies and Deadlines

Sometimes students worry their work has been treated unfairly by their instructors. If you feel like this has happened, start by carefully reviewing your instructor's comments, the assignment instructions, and the grade guidelines in this book. Then make an appointment to talk to your instructor. If reviewing the materials and talking to your instructor doesn't help answer your questions or concerns, then the English 1010 program at UW has a formal grade appeal process in place.

Our process aligns with and follows the appeal policies of UW's College of Arts and Sciences. Their "Student Appeals Guidelines and Procedures" are published online. To argue that a grade should be appealed, you must demonstrate the grade is "prejudice" or "capricious." In other words, your argument must be based on an assertion that you were not treated like other students in the class (so you can't argue that the instructor is "too strict" if that same strictness was applied to everyone).

If you plan to appeal a grade, then you *must* contact your instructor *in writing* and ask for the grade to be reconsidered. That requirement is part of the policies for the college and for the department. For an assignment graded during the middle of the term, the request should be sent *within ten weekdays* of receiving the grade. If you want to appeal your final grade, then you must make the request to your instructor *within 10 work days* of the start of the following term. If your instructor is no longer at the university and/or if you want more details about the department or college policies and procedures, please contact the Director of Writing Programs through the English department.

If you are not satisfied with the outcomes after talking with your instructor, then contact the Director of Writing Programs or the Department Chair for the next steps. Do this within one week of hearing back from your instructor.

Feedback and Grading

How Instructors Give Feedback in ENGL 1010

ENGL 1010 uses a portfolio approach to grade student writing: this means that your instructor responds to your writing in various stages of progress, *and* that you may revise your work until the very last day of class. You will also have multiple opportunities to get feedback from your classmates, and are encouraged to seek feedback from Writing Center tutors, fellow students, and campus support services.

The portfolio system ensures that you have plenty of time to get feedback on, reimagine, revise, and polish your writing. Instructor comments on early drafts may include a good faith estimate of the potential grade of a draft in progress, but such comments have absolutely no bearing on the grade you receive on your course portfolio. Instead, a team of instructors grades your portfolio holistically based on the quality of the work you submit at midterm and at the end of the semester.

At the end of each assignment, you will turn in a polished draft and your instructor will carefully respond to it, noting what you have done well, possible strategies for improvement, and your draft's potential for success in the course portfolio.

Portfolio Team Grading

Your midterm and final portfolio will be evaluated by your classroom instructor and at least one additional ENGL 1010 instructor. If these two instructors do not agree on the same letter grade, then a third instructor will evaluate your portfolio and help the team come to consensus. The team grading system brings instructors together for productive small-group discussions of teaching and grading throughout the term, allows instructors to coach students as they draft and revise their writing, and ensures that the grades students receive are representative of the common standards endorsed by the First Year Writing Program as a whole.

At or before midterm, you will submit a midterm portfolio to get a sense of what it is like to be evaluated by a team of instructors. Midterm portfolios are graded with a simple letter grade (A, B, C, D, or F) and your classroom instructor will adjust your midterm grade by a plus, a minus, or no adjustment to reflect the degree your writing has improved over time.

At the end of the semester, you will submit a final portfolio, which includes revised versions of a selection of major writing assignments. Final portfolios are graded with a simple letter grade and your classroom instructor will adjust your final portfolio grade with a plus, minus, or no adjustment to reflect the degree your writing has improved over time.

Classroom Participation and Oral and Multimodal Presentations

Your classroom participation and oral presentations will be holistically evaluated by your instructor based on appropriate participation guidelines, which include: the quality and consistency of your contributions to class discussions and activities, timely and satisfactory engagement in and completion of assignments and readings, and the quality of your oral presentations. Your classroom participation and oral presentations grade is also influenced by factors such as consistent attendance—you can't do well if you don't show up regularly.

Frequently Asked Questions (and Answers) About Grading in English 1010

1. **When I hand in drafts of my work, my instructor's comments suggest that my writing is much weaker now than it was in high school. For example, I took Honors English and earned an A, but my English 1010 instructor thinks my draft is closer to the C range. Was my teacher in high school wrong or is my college instructor?**

   Answer: Neither, actually. The writing conventions high school teachers teach, the goals they set for students, and the standards they use to grade student work are different than the conventions, goals, and standards of university instructors. That's appropriate, because the goal of a high school education is to ensure adolescents are prepared to function as adults, while the goal of a college education is to ensure adults have mastery of academic subject matter and conventions. One of the primary goals of English 1010 is to make you aware of new expectations for your writing, to prepare you to succeed *at the university level*. Use your English 1010 instructor's comments to set goals for your next draft and for future writing assignments. While comments on early drafts may sting, it's your instructor's job to point out where you can improve, to coach, and to help motivate you to produce writing that satisfies academic conventions. Remember, too, that you have time to revise your work before submitting it for a final grade in your portfolio. Don't be hard on yourself (or your instructors!) and don't let an unexpected comment about the quality of your work discourage you. Instead, visit your instructor during office hours, visit the Writing Center, and start revising.

2. **Why is a team of English 1010 instructors evaluating my portfolio rather than just my own instructor?**

   Answer: A group of four or more instructors (including your own) has been reading samples of your class's writing throughout the semester to discuss and agree about what constitutes A, B, C, D, and F writing. The goal of the group is to create clear and fair grading standards that instructors communicate and reinforce in their classrooms. One advantage of our team grading system is that it protects English 1010 students from being misled by "easy" graders or penalized by "hard" graders. When you leave this course, you should have an accurate sense of what you do well, areas for improvement, and how your writing measures up to the university community's standards.

3. **Does my instructor have any say on my grade in English 1010 and my portfolio?**

    Answer: Yes. Your instructor will always be one of at least two readers of your portfolio. If the second reader in the group agrees with your instructor, then the grade your instructor gave your portfolio is the grade you will receive. (First and second readers agree about 70–80% of the time.) If the second reader does not agree with your instructor, then a third reader will join the conversation and help the other readers come to consensus on a fair grade. Rather than grading in isolation and without the guidance and support of other members of the university community, English 1010 instructors work together to ensure that the grade you receive is in keeping with standards agreed upon by our academic community.

4. **What happens if one person in the portfolio group grades much harder than the others? Doesn't this mean I'll get a lower grade?**

    Answer: No, not in this system. If the first two readers of your portfolio don't agree on a grade, a third reader is asked to read your portfolio and decide what grade is most in line with the standards agreed upon by the team of graders. So if one reader does have unreasonable standards, the other two readers will help determine an appropriate grade.

5. **I think each instructor should grade his or her own students' work. Why can't I choose?**

    Answer: Each instructor does have a hand in grading student work: all instructors serve as the first reader in a multi-reader grading system. What's more, your instructor alone evaluates your performance on oral presentations and classroom participation, which constitute 20% of your course grade.

6. **My instructor said that I have to meet specific guidelines that are particular to my section of English 1010. If other instructors in the grading group have different guidelines, are they going to penalize me?**

    Answer: No. Instructors often have minimum requirements they want every paper to meet. For example, some instructors require students to use particular kinds of research sources, while others may ask students to approach one of the major assignments in an innovative way. When instructors have different requirements, they communicate them clearly to other members of the grading group.

7. **Just looking at my portfolio at the end of the term doesn't show how much I've improved. Shouldn't my grade be based, at least in part, on my improvement?**

    Answer: Yes, we agree that it should. That's why instructors adjust the portfolio grade with a plus or minus (or make no adjustment) given your hard work and improvement. Improvement in your writing over time can and does positively influence your grade in the course.

8. **I like to have grades during the semester so that I know how well I am doing. I don't want my grade at the end of the term to come as a big surprise. Why don't I receive grades throughout the semester?**

    Answer: We don't want you to be surprised either. Your instructor should be reading your writing throughout the semester and responding to it with written comments and in personal conferences. Your instructor should provide feedback about what you are doing well and should make suggestions for improvement. In providing feedback, your instructor should 1) indicate what other instructors in the same grading group have been saying about writing like yours, and 2) discuss what grade characteristics your drafts-in-progress embody. Still, if you're concerned about the status of your grade or have questions about the quality of your work, don't hesitate to schedule additional conferences with your instructor. If you feel you aren't getting satisfactory feedback, please discuss your concerns with your instructor, or contact the English Department to make an appointment with the Director of Writing Programs.

9. **The grading team read my final course portfolio but didn't give me feedback. Why not?**

    Answer: Your instructor has given you written feedback on drafts as well as opportunities to discuss your work in a variety of classroom, office hour, and Writing Center settings. At the end of the semester, because there are no longer opportunities for revision, grading teams are focused on determining your grade, not on giving you feedback. Your instructor is helping to set standards in the grading group throughout the semester, so take this feedback seriously and work hard to implement it in your writing. Student who pass the course generally don't receive written feedback on the portfolio, although instructors do send an explanation of your course grade if you do not earn a C in the course. Of course, if you feel there may have been an error or have questions about your course grade after the semester ends, please contact your instructor. Sometimes mistakes happen.

10. **Can I include a paper in my portfolio from another class or from high school?**

    Answer: No. All papers in your portfolio must have been assigned and written in this semester of English 1010 instruction. Students who submit work from another class or submit work not previously reviewed by the instructor not only risk facing academic dishonesty charges, they will receive an F for the course.

11. **What do I do if I have questions about my final grade? Can I get a report on how my course grade was calculated?**

    Answer: If you have questions about how your instructor arrived at your final grade, contact your instructor via email and request to see your percentage breakdown for your final portfolio grade and your presentation and classroom participation grade. After you receive a response, if you still have questions, concerns, or believe there may have been an error in calculating your grade, please contact the English Department. The Director of Writing Programs will be happy to follow up on your situation.

12. **It seems to me that the portfolio grading system is all about judging final products. I thought we were supposed to be interested in the writing process. What gives?**

    Answer: We use portfolio team grading to respond to the university community's desire to ensure that entry-level students understand and have the opportunity to study and practice college writing conventions before moving on to upper-division courses. We want you to be prepared for the challenging writing assignments you'll face throughout your four years at the University of Wyoming. So yes, English 1010 focuses primarily on writing process strategies that will help you succeed as a college writer, but that doesn't mean we don't have high expectations for your writing. After all, not only do you have an entire semester to revise your work for the final portfolio, but the university community wants you to strive for excellence. We know you're up to the challenge, so stay focused and keep revising!

Grading Criteria for Writing

Characteristics of "A" Writing: Outstanding Writing

Content
- A single focus is emphasized through the entire paper, and is developed with significant and interesting details, examples, and discussion.
- Research sources are relevant and mainly academic or professional in nature, and are clearly introduced and integrated into the discussion.
- The writing artfully fulfills the assignment criteria.

Audience
- The material challenges the intelligence and sophistication of a college audience, and is clear to readers beyond the writer's classroom.
- Word choice is precise, interesting, and appropriate to the writing task.
- The language is mature and idiomatic.
- The tone complements the writer's purpose and suits the audience.

Organization
- The overall pattern is artfully conceived.
- The argument or focus of the paper is clearly emphasized.
- The focus is developed through a sequence of related paragraphs.
- Paragraphs are purposefully organized and substantially developed with supporting evidence or detailed examples.
- The opening and closing are inviting, challenging, and appropriate.
- Transitions between and within paragraphs are explicit, clear, and purposeful.

Conventions
- Sentence structure varies according to the content and purpose of the assignment.
- Sentences are clear, logical, and enjoyable to read.
- References to sources are cited and documented using the citation system discussed in class.
- Problems in grammar, spelling, punctuation, or usage do not interfere with communication.
- As applicable, elements of digital design reflect careful attention to conventions and detail.

Characteristics of "B" Writing: Strong Writing

Content

- The focus is developed with appropriate details, examples, and discussion.
- Research sources are relevant and are clearly introduced and integrated into discussion.
- The writing clearly fulfills the assignment criteria.

Audience

- The material is thoughtful and engaging to a college audience, and is clear to readers beyond the writer's classroom.
- Word choice and vocabulary are appropriate to the writing task.
- The language is idiomatic.
- The tone is appropriate to the writer's purpose and audience.

Organization

- The overall pattern is clear and sensible.
- The argument or focus is clearly identifiable.
- The focus is developed through a sequence of related paragraphs.
- Paragraphs are clearly organized, but some may lack richness of detail or evidence.
- The opening and closing are appropriate to the focus.
- Transitions between and within paragraphs advance the writer's ideas.

Conventions

- Sentences are varied in structure, and only rarely choppy or repetitive.
- Sentences are generally clear, logical, and readable.
- References to sources are generally cited and documented using the citation system discussed in class.
- Problems in grammar, spelling, punctuation, or usage rarely interfere with communication.
- As applicable, elements of digital design reflect attention to conventions and detail.

Characteristics of "C" Writing: Writing that Meets Expectations

Content

- The focus is generally developed with details, examples, and discussion.
- Research sources are generally relevant, although not always clearly introduced or integrated into the discussion.
- Paragraphs tend to lack richness of evidence or detailed examples.
- The writing reasonably fulfills most assignment criteria, though minor aspects of the assignment may be missing, unclear, or underdeveloped.

Audience

- The material is reasonable, but may not fully engage a college audience; sections may be unclear to those outside the writer's classroom.
- Although most words are well-chosen, some may not be as precise or apt as they could be.
- Occasional lapses from standard idioms occur.
- The tone, though generally consistent, at times appears inappropriate to the writer's purpose and audience.

Organization

- The writer establishes an overall pattern for the paper to follow.
- An argument or focus runs through the paper, although parts wander from the central idea.
- The argument or focus is identifiable.
- The focus is generally developed throughout the paper, although some paragraphs may appear out of sequence or slightly off-track.
- The opening and closing generally support the topic and focus.
- Transitions are evident, but may be abrupt or mechanical.

Conventions

- Sentences are sometimes basic, choppy, or structurally repetitive.
- Sentences are generally readable, but ideas may be hard to follow from one section to the next.
- References to sources are generally cited and documented, but not always according to the citation system discussed in class.
- Problems in grammar, spelling, punctuation, or usage occasionally interfere with communication and impair the writer's credibility.
- As applicable, elements of digital design reflect some attention to conventions, though details are sometimes inconsistent.

Characteristics of "D" Writing: Writing that Does Not Meet Expectations

Content

- A focus may be stated, but is not developed with details, examples, and discussion.
- Research sources may be irrelevant or misinterpreted and/or are often not clearly introduced or integrated.
- The writing does not fulfill important assignment criteria, and major aspects of the assignment may be missing, unclear, or underdeveloped.

Audience

- The material does not fully engage the abilities of a college audience, or is unclear to those outside the writer's classroom.
- The reader must reread many sentences in order to comprehend them.
- The writer displays inadequate control of diction; word-choice problems are frequent, as are problems with standard idioms.
- The tone frequently appears inappropriate to the purpose and audience.

Organization

- The writer hasn't established a clear pattern for the paper to follow.
- The argument or focus is overly general, missing, or unclear.
- An attempt at focus development may be evident, but is unsuccessful.
- Paragraphs frequently seem unrelated or repetitive, are poorly constructed, and/or contain little supporting detail.
- The opening and closing are overly general, missing, or misleading.
- Transitions are weak, ineffective, or missing.

Conventions

- Sentences are frequently basic, choppy, or repetitive.
- Sentence problems impede effective communication.
- Many errors in spelling, grammar, punctuation, and usage impede communication and damage the writer's credibility.
- References to sources are not clearly cited; documentation consistently ignores the citation system discussed in class.
- As applicable, elements of digital design reflect little attention to conventions or detail.

Characteristics of "F" Writing

- In addition to many "D" characteristics, the writing does not fulfill minimum assignment criteria, including word count requirements, source integration expectations, submission of process drafts, and the like.

Grading Criteria for Classroom Participation and Oral Presentations

Characteristics of "A" or Outstanding Class Participation and Oral Presentations

Classroom Participation

- The student attends nearly every class period on time.
- The student contributes fruitfully, appropriately, and frequently to class discussions.
- The student completes all assignments and readings conscientiously and on time.
- The student actively and enthusiastically participates in all class activities.
- The student always provides thoughtful and substantial feedback to peers during presentations, workshops, and activities.
- The student always actively listens and responds to peers and the instructor.

Oral Presentations

- The material challenges the intelligence and sophistication of a college audience, and would be clear to audiences beyond the student's classroom.
- The focus of each presentation is clearly emphasized.
- Presentations are purposefully organized and substantially developed with supporting evidence or detailed examples.
- The openings and closings are inviting, challenging, and appropriate.
- The student exhibits a sophisticated attention to the basics of oral communication including eye contact, clarity, delivery speed and volume, time requirements, and overall professionalism.
- The presentations artfully fulfill the assignment criteria.

Characteristics of "B" or Strong Class Participation and Oral Presentations

Classroom Participation

- The student attends a vast majority of class periods and is rarely late.
- The student contributes productively and consistently to class discussions.
- The student regularly completes assignments and readings well and on time.
- The student actively participates in class activities.
- The student consistently provides thoughtful feedback to peers during presentations, workshops, and activities.
- The student actively listens and responds to peers and the instructor.

Oral Presentations

- The material is thoughtful and engaging to a college audience, and would be clear to audiences beyond the student's classroom.
- A single focus runs through each presentation.
- The focus of each presentation is developed through supporting evidence or detailed examples.
- The openings and closings are appropriate.
- The student successfully exhibits the basics of oral communication, including eye contact, clarity, delivery speed and volume, time requirements, and overall professionalism.
- The presentations clearly fulfill the assignment criteria.

Characteristics of "C" or Satisfactory Classroom Participation and Oral Presentations

Classroom Participation

- The student attends most class periods, though is occasionally late.
- The student sometimes contributes productively to class discussions.
- The student completes most assignments and readings satisfactorily and on time.
- The student participates in class activities.
- The student generally provides thoughtful feedback during presentations, workshops, and activities.
- The student pays attention in class and listens to peers and the instructor.

Oral Presentations

- The material is reasonable but may not fully engage a college audience; portions of the presentations may be unclear to audiences beyond the student's classroom.
- A single focus runs through each presentation, although parts may wander from the central idea.
- The focus of each presentation is generally developed throughout the presentation, though some information may seem slightly off-track.
- The openings and closings generally support the topic and focus.
- The student satisfactorily exhibits most of the basics of oral communication though some areas are performed less satisfactorily than others.
- The presentations reasonably fulfill most of the assignment criteria.

Characteristics of "D" or Unsatisfactory Class Participation and Oral Presentations

Classroom Participation

- The student is routinely absent and/or routinely late to class.
- The student rarely and/or inconsistently contributes to class discussions.
- The student completes some assignments and readings well and on time, but many are late, incomplete, or not performed at all.
- The student participates in some class activities, though often stays silent during discussion or does not actively contribute to group activities.
- The student seldom provides thoughtful and substantial feedback to peers during presentations, workshops, and activities.
- The student is routinely distracted during class, or may occasionally even seek to distract others.

Oral Presentations

- The material does not fully engage a college audience, or is unclear to audiences beyond the student's classroom.
- The focus of each presentation is overly general, missing, or unclear.
- The student hasn't established a clear pattern for the presentation to follow.
- The openings and closings are overly general, missing, or misleading.
- The student does not exhibit many of the basics of oral communication including eye contact, clarity, delivery speed and volume, time requirements, and overall professionalism.
- The presentations fail to fulfill several of the assignment criteria.

Characteristics of "F" or Failing Class Participation and Oral Presentations

- In addition to reflecting many "D" characteristics, the student does not fulfill basic classroom expectations and/or assignment criteria, and exceeds the number of allowable absences.

Section One

Introduction to College-Level Writing

Because our course teaches writing through a genre-based approach, the first two readings introduce more details about academic writing in general and genres more specifically. "What is 'Academic' Writing?" gets us all on the same page regarding course expectations. In particular, the sections on the myths about writing and on the types of assignments may help you think about questions to ask instructors in classes even beyond English 1010. The word "genre" can sometimes be confusing, but the storytelling and fun examples in "Navigating Genres" make understanding form and features a bit easier. Together, these two readings provide the foundation for the rest of the course. Make sure to check out the list of questions following these readings—these are intended to help you think about your work and may inspire discussion in class and/or in your instructor conferences.

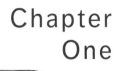

Chapter One

What Is "Academic" Writing?
by L. Lennie Irvin

Introduction: The Academic Writing Task

As a new college student, you may have a lot of anxiety and questions about the writing you'll do in college. That word "academic," especially, may turn your stomach or turn your nose. However, with this first year composition class, you begin one of the only classes in your entire college career where you will focus on learning to write. Given the importance of writing as a communication skill, I urge you to consider this class as a gift and make the most of it. But writing is hard, and writing in college may resemble playing a familiar game by completely new rules (that often are unstated). This chapter is designed to introduce you to what academic writing is like, and hopefully ease your transition as you face these daunting writing challenges.

So here's the secret. Your success with academic writing depends upon how well you understand what you are doing as you write and then how you approach the writing task. Early research done on college writers discovered that whether students produced a successful piece of writing depended largely upon their representation of the writing task. The writers' mental model for picturing their task made a huge difference. Most people as they start college have wildly strange ideas about what they are doing when they write an essay, or worse—they have no clear idea at all. I freely admit my

"What Is 'Academic' Writing?" by L. Lennie Irvin. *Writing Spaces: Readings on Writing*, Volume 1. http://writingspaces.org/sites/default/files/irvin--what-is-academic-writing.pdf

own past as a clueless freshman writer, and it's out of this sympathy as well as twenty years of teaching college writing that I hope to provide you with something useful. So grab a cup of coffee or a diet coke, find a comfortable chair with good light, and let's explore together this activity of academic writing you'll be asked to do in college. We will start by clearing up some of those wild misconceptions people often arrive at college possessing. Then we will dig more deeply into the components of the academic writing situation and nature of the writing task.

Myths About Writing

Though I don't imagine an episode of *MythBusters* will be based on the misconceptions about writing we are about to look at, you'd still be surprised at some of the things people will believe about writing. You may find lurking within you viral elements of these myths—all of these lead to problems in writing.

Myth #1: The "Paint by Numbers" myth

Some writers believe they must perform certain steps in a particular order to write "correctly." Rather than being a lock-step linear process, writing is "recursive." That means we cycle through and repeat the various activities of the writing process many times as we write.

Myth #2: Writers only start writing when they have everything figured out

Writing is not like sending a fax! Writers figure out much of what they want to write as they write it. Rather than waiting, get some writing on the page—even with gaps or problems. You can come back to patch up rough spots.

Myth #3: Perfect first drafts

We put unrealistic expectations on early drafts, either by focusing too much on the impossible task of making them perfect (which can put a cap on the development of our ideas), or by making too little effort because we don't care or know about their inevitable problems. Nobody writes perfect first drafts; polished writing takes lots of revision.

Myth #4: Some got it; I don't—the genius fallacy

When you see your writing ability as something fixed or out of your control (as if it were in your genetic code), then you won't believe you can improve as a writer and are likely not to make any efforts in that direction. With effort and study, though, you can improve as a writer. I promise.

Myth #5: Good grammar is good writing

When people say "I can't write," what they often mean is they have problems with grammatical correctness. Writing, however, is about more than just grammatical correctness. Good writing is a matter of achieving your desired effect upon an intended audience. Plus, as we saw in myth #3, no one writes perfect first drafts.

Myth #6: The Five Paragraph Essay

Some people say to avoid it at all costs, while others believe no other way to write exists. With an introduction, three supporting paragraphs, and a conclusion, the five paragraph essay is a format you should know, but one which you will outgrow. You'll have to gauge the particular writing assignment to see whether and how this format is useful for you.

Myth #7: Never use "I"

Adopting this formal stance of objectivity implies a distrust (almost fear) of informality and often leads to artificial, puffed-up prose. Although some writing situations will call on you to avoid using "I" (for example, a lab report), much college writing can be done in a middle, semi-formal style where it is ok to use "I."

The Academic Writing Situation

Now that we've dispelled some of the common myths that many writers have as they enter a college classroom, let's take a moment to think about the academic writing situation. The biggest problem I see in freshman writers is a poor sense of the writing situation in general. To illustrate this problem, let's look at the difference between speaking and writing.

When we speak, we inhabit the communication situation bodily in three dimensions, but in writing we are confined within the two-dimensional setting of the flat page (though writing for the web—or multimodal writing—is changing all that). Writing resembles having a blindfold over our eyes and our hands tied behind our backs: we can't see exactly whom we're talking to or where we are. Separated from our audience in place and time, we imaginatively have to create this context. Our words on the page are silent, so we must use punctuation and word choice to communicate our tone. We also can't see our audience to gauge how our communication is being received or if there will be some kind of response. It's the same space we share right now as you read this essay. Novice writers often write as if they were mumbling to themselves in the corner with no sense that their writing will be read by a reader or any sense of the context within which their communication will be received.

What's the moral here? Developing your "writer's sense" about communicating within the writing situation is the most important thing you should learn in freshman composition.

Figure 1, depicting the writing situation, presents the best image I know of describing all the complexities involved in the writing situation.

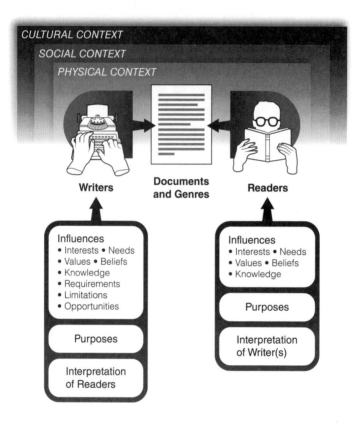

Figure 1. Source: "A Social Model of Writing." Writing@CSU. 2010.

Looking More Closely at the "Academic Writing" Situation

Writing in college is a fairly specialized writing situation, and it has developed its own codes and conventions that you need to have a keen awareness of if you are going to write successfully in college. Let's break down the writing situation in college:

Who's your audience?	Primarily the professor and possibly your classmates (though you may be asked to include a secondary outside audience).
What's the occasion or context?	An assignment given by the teacher within a learning context and designed to have you learn and demonstrate your learning.
What's your message?	It will be your learning or the interpretation gained from your study of the subject matter.
What's your purpose?	To show your learning and get a good grade (or to accomplish the goals of the writing assignment).
What documents/genres are used?	The essay is the most frequent type of document used.

So far, this list looks like nothing new. You've been writing in school toward teachers for years. What's different in college? Lee Ann Carroll, a professor at Pepperdine University, performed a study of student writing in college and had this description of the kind of writing you will be doing in college:

What are usually called 'writing assignments' in college might more accurately be called 'literacy tasks' because they require much more than the ability to construct correct sentences or compose neatly organized paragraphs with topic sentences... Projects calling for high levels of critical literacy in college typically require knowledge of research skills, ability to read complex texts, understanding of key disciplinary concepts, and strategies for synthesizing, analyzing, and responding critically to new information, usually within a limited time frame. (3–4)

Academic writing is always a form of evaluation that asks you to demonstrate knowledge and show proficiency with certain disciplinary skills of thinking, interpreting, and presenting. Writing the paper is never "just" the writing part. To be successful in this kind of writing, you must be completely aware of what the professor expects you to do and accomplish with that particular writing task. For a moment, let's explore more deeply the elements of this college writing "literacy task."

Knowledge of Research Skills

Perhaps up to now research has meant going straight to Google and Wikipedia, but college will require you to search for and find more in-depth information. You'll need to know how to find information in the library, especially what is available from online databases which contain scholarly articles. Researching is also a process, so you'll need to learn how to focus and direct a research project and how to keep track of all your source information. Realize that researching represents a crucial component of most all college writing assignments, and you will need to devote lots of work to this researching.

The Ability to Read Complex Texts

Whereas your previous writing in school might have come generally from your experience, college writing typically asks you to write on unfamiliar topics. Whether you're reading your textbook, a short story, or scholarly articles from research, your ability to write well will be based upon the quality of your reading. In addition to the labor of close reading, you'll need to think critically as you read. That means separating fact from opinion, recognizing biases and assumptions, and making inferences. Inferences are how we as readers connect the dots: an inference is a belief (or statement) about something unknown made on the basis of something known. You smell smoke; you infer fire. They are conclusions or interpretations that we arrive at based upon the known factors we discover from our reading. When we, then, write to argue for these interpretations, our job becomes to get our readers to make the same inferences we have made.

The Understanding of Key Disciplinary Concepts

Each discipline whether it is English, Psychology, or History has its own key concepts and language for describing these important ways of understanding the world. Don't fool yourself that your professors' writing assignments are asking for your opinion on the topic from just your experience. They want to see you apply and use these concepts in your writing. Though different from a multiple-choice exam, writing similarly requires you to demonstrate your learning. So whatever writing assignment you receive, inspect it closely for what concepts it asks you to bring into your writing.

Strategies for Synthesizing, Analyzing, and Responding Critically to New Information

You need to develop the skill of a seasoned traveler who can be dropped in any city around the world and get by. Each writing assignment asks you to navigate through a new terrain of information, so you must develop ways for grasping new subject matter in order, then, to use it in your writing. We have already seen the importance of reading and research for these literacy tasks, but beyond laying the information out before you, you will need to learn ways of sorting and finding meaningful patterns in this information.

In College, Everything's an Argument: A Guide for Decoding College Writing Assignments

Let's restate this complex "literacy task" you'll be asked repeatedly to do in your writing assignments. Typically, you'll be required to write an "essay" based upon your analysis of some reading(s). In this essay you'll need to present an argument where you make a claim (i.e. present a "thesis") and support that claim with good reasons that have adequate and appropriate evidence to back them up. The dynamic of this argumentative task often confuses first year writers, so let's examine it more closely.

Academic Writing Is an Argument

To start, let's focus on argument. What does it mean to present an "argument" in college writing? Rather than a shouting match between two disagreeing sides, argument instead means a carefully arranged and supported presentation of a viewpoint. Its purpose is not so much to win the argument as to earn your audience's consideration (and even approval) of your perspective. It resembles a conversation between two people who may not hold the same opinions, but they both desire a better understanding of the subject matter under discussion. My favorite analogy, however, to describe the nature of this argumentative stance in college writing is the courtroom. In this scenario, you are like a lawyer making a case at trial that the defendant is not guilty, and your readers are like the jury who will decide if the defendant is guilty or not guilty. This jury (your readers) won't just take your word that he's innocent; instead, you must convince them by presenting evidence that proves he is not guilty. Stating your opinion is not enough—you have to back it up too. I like this courtroom analogy for capturing two importance things about academic argument: 1) the value of an organized presentation of your "case," and 2) the crucial element of strong evidence.

Academic Writing Is an Analysis

We now turn our attention to the actual writing assignment and that confusing word "analyze." Your first job when you get a writing assignment is to figure out what the professor expects. This assignment may be explicit in its expectations, but often built into the wording of the most defined writing assignments are implicit expectations that you might not recognize. First, we can say that unless your professor specifically asks you to summarize, you won't write a summary. Let me say that again: don't write a summary unless directly asked to. But what, then, does the professor want? We have already picked out a few of these expectations: You can count on the instructor expecting you to read closely, research adequately, and write an argument where you will demonstrate your ability to apply and use important concepts you have been studying. But the writing task also implies that your essay will be the result of an analysis. At times, the writing assignment may even explicitly say to write an analysis, but often this element of the task remains unstated.

So what does it mean to analyze? One way to think of an analysis is that it asks you to seek How and Why questions much more than What questions. An analysis involves doing three things:

1. Engage in an open inquiry where the answer is not known at first (and where you leave yourself open to multiple suggestions).

2. Identify meaningful parts of the subject.

3. Examine these separate parts and determine how they relate to each other.

An analysis breaks a subject apart to study it closely, and from this inspection, ideas for writing emerge. When writing assignments call on you to analyze, they require you to identify the parts of the subject (parts of an ad, parts of a short story, parts of Hamlet's character), and then show how these parts fit or don't fit together to create some larger effect or meaning. Your interpretation of how these parts fit together constitutes your claim or thesis, and the task of your essay is then to present an argument defending your interpretation as a valid or plausible one to make. My biggest bit of advice about analysis is not to do it all in your head. Analysis works best when you put all the cards on the table, so to speak. Identify and isolate the parts of your analysis, and record important features and characteristics of each one. As patterns emerge, you sort and connect these parts in meaningful ways. For me, I have always had to do this recording and thinking on scratch pieces of paper. Just as critical reading forms a crucial element of the literacy task of a college writing assignment, so too does this analysis process. It's built in.

Three Common Types of College Writing Assignments

We have been decoding the expectations of the academic writing task so far, and I want to turn now to examine the types of assignments you might receive. From my experience, you are likely to get three kinds of writing assignments based upon the instructor's degree of direction for the assignment. We'll take a brief look at each kind of academic writing task.

The Closed Writing Assignment

*   Is Creon a character to admire or condemn?

*   Does your advertisement employ techniques of propaganda, and if so what kind?

*   Was the South justified in seceding from the Union?

*   In your opinion, do you believe Hamlet was truly mad?

These kinds of writing assignments present you with two counter claims and ask you to determine from your own analysis the more valid claim. They resemble yes-no questions. These topics define the claim for you, so the major task of the writing assignment then is working out the support for the claim. They resemble a math problem in which the teacher has given you the answer and now wants you to "show your work" in arriving at that answer.

Be careful with these writing assignments, however, because often these topics don't have a simple yes/no, either/or answer (despite the nature of the essay question). A close analysis of the subject matter often reveals nuances and ambiguities within the question that your eventual claim should reflect. Perhaps a claim such as, "In my opinion, Hamlet was mad" might work, but I urge you to avoid such a simplistic thesis. This thesis would be better: "I believe Hamlet's unhinged mind borders on insanity but doesn't quite reach it."

The Semi-Open Writing Assignment

- Discuss the role of law in *Antigone*.

- Explain the relationship between character and fate in *Hamlet*.

- Compare and contrast the use of setting in two short stories.

- Show how the Fugitive Slave Act influenced the Abolitionist Movement.

Although these topics chart out a subject matter for you to write upon, they don't offer up claims you can easily use in your paper. It would be a misstep to offer up claims such as, "Law plays a role in *Antigone*" or "In *Hamlet* we can see a relationship between character and fate." Such statements express the obvious and what the topic takes for granted. The question, for example, is not whether law plays a role in *Antigone*, but rather what sort of role law plays. What is the nature of this role? What influences does it have on the characters or actions or theme? This kind of writing assignment resembles a kind of archeological dig. The teacher cordons off an area, hands you a shovel, and says dig here and see what you find.

Be sure to avoid summary and mere explanation in this kind of assignment. Despite using key words in the assignment such as "explain," "illustrate," "analyze," "discuss," or "show how," these topics still ask you to make an argument. Implicit in the topic is the expectation that you will analyze the reading and arrive at some insights into patterns and relationships about the subject. Your eventual paper, then, needs to present what you found from this analysis—the treasure you found from your digging. Determining your own claim represents the biggest challenge for this type of writing assignment.

The Open Writing Assignment

* Analyze the role of a character in Dante's *Inferno*.

* What does it mean to be an "American" in the 21st Century?

* Analyze the influence of slavery upon one cause of the Civil War.

* Compare and contrast two themes within *Pride and Prejudice*.

These kinds of writing assignments require you to decide both your writing topic and your claim (or thesis). Which character in the *Inferno* will I pick to analyze? What two themes in *Pride and Prejudice* will I choose to write about? Many students struggle with these types of assignments because they have to understand their subject matter well before they can intelligently choose a topic. For instance, you need a good familiarity with the characters in the *Inferno* before you can pick one. You have to have a solid understanding defining elements of American identity as well as 21st century culture before you can begin to connect them. This kind of writing assignment resembles riding a bike without the training wheels on. It says, "You decide what to write about." The biggest decision, then, becomes selecting your topic and limiting it to a manageable size.

Picking and Limiting a Writing Topic

Let's talk about both of these challenges: picking a topic and limiting it. Remember how I said these kinds of essay topics expect you to choose what to write about from a solid understanding of your subject? As you read and review your subject matter, look for things that interest you. Look for gaps, puzzling items, things that confuse you, or connections you see. Something in this pile of rocks should stand out as a jewel: as being "doable" and interesting. (You'll write best when you write from both your head and your heart.) Whatever topic you choose, state it as a clear and interesting question. You may or may not state this essay question explicitly in the introduction of your paper (I actually recommend that you do), but it will provide direction for your paper and a focus for your claim since that claim will be your answer to this essay question. For example, if with the Dante topic you decided to write on Virgil, your essay question might be: "What is the role of Virgil toward the character of Dante in the *Inferno*?" The thesis statement, then, might be this: "Virgil's predominant role as Dante's guide through hell is as the voice of reason." Crafting a solid essay question is well worth your time because it charts the territory of your essay and helps you declare a focused thesis statement.

Many students struggle with defining the right size for their writing project. They chart out an essay question that it would take a book to deal with adequately. You'll know you have that kind of topic if you have already written over the required page length but only touched one quarter of the topics you planned to discuss. In this case, carve out one of those topics and make your whole paper about it. For instance, with our Dante example, perhaps you planned to discuss four places where Virgil's role as the voice of reason is evident. Instead of discussing all four, focus your essay on just one place. So your revised thesis statement might be: "Close inspection of Cantos I and II reveal that Virgil serves predominantly as the voice of reason for Dante on his journey through hell." A writing teacher I had in college said it this way: A well-tended garden is better than a large one full of weeds. That means to limit your topic to a size you can handle and support well.

Three Characteristics of Academic Writing

I want to wrap up this section by sharing in broad terms what the expectations are behind an academic writing assignment. Chris Thaiss and Terry Zawacki conducted research at George Mason University where they asked professors from their university what they thought academic writing was and its standards. They came up with three characteristics:

1. Clear evidence in writing that the writer(s) have been persistent, open-minded, and disciplined in study. (5)

2. The dominance of reason over emotions or sensual perception. (5)

3. An imagined reader who is coolly rational, reading for information, and intending to formulate a reasoned response. (7)

Your professor wants to see these three things in your writing when they give you a writing assignment. They want to see in your writing the results of your efforts at the various literacy tasks we have been discussing: critical reading, research, and analysis. Beyond merely stating opinions, they also want to see an argument toward an intelligent audience where you provide good reasons to support your interpretations.

The Format of the Academic Essay

Your instructors will also expect you to deliver a paper that contains particular textual features. The following list contains the characteristics of what I have for years called the "critical essay." Although I can't claim they will be useful for all essays in college, I hope that these features will help you shape and accomplish successful college essays. Be aware that these characteristics are flexible and not a formula, and any particular assignment might ask for something different.

Characteristics of the Critical Essay

"Critical" here is not used in the sense of "to criticize" as in find fault with. Instead, "critical" is used in the same way "critical thinking" is used. A synonym might be "interpretive" or "analytical."

1. It is an argument, persuasion essay that in its broadest sense MAKES A POINT and SUPPORTS IT. (We have already discussed this argumentative nature of academic writing at length.)

2. The point ("claim" or "thesis") of a critical essay is interpretive in nature. That means the point is debatable and open to interpretation, not a statement of the obvious. The thesis statement is a clear, declarative sentence that often works best when it comes at the end of the introduction.

3. Organization: Like any essay, the critical essay should have a clear introduction, body, and conclusion. As you support your point in the body of the essay, you should "divide up the proof," which means structuring the body around clear primary supports (developed in single paragraphs for short papers or multiple paragraphs for longer papers).

4. Support: (a) The primary source for support in the critical essay is from the text (or sources). The text is the authority, so using quotations is required. (b) The continuous movement of logic in a critical essay is "assert then support; assert then support." No assertion (general statement that needs proving) should be left without specific support (often from the text(s)). (c) You need enough support to be convincing. In general, that means for each assertion you need at least three supports. This threshold can vary, but invariably one support is not enough.

5. A critical essay will always "document" its sources, distinguishing the use of outside information used inside your text and clarifying where that information came from (following the rules of MLA documentation style or whatever documentation style is required).

6. Whenever the author moves from one main point (primary support) to the next, the author needs to clearly signal to the reader that this movement is happening. This transition sentence works best when it links back to the thesis as it states the topic of that paragraph or section.

7. A critical essay is put into an academic essay format such as the MLA or APA document format.

8. Grammatical correctness: Your essay should have few if any grammatical problems. You'll want to edit your final draft carefully before turning it in.

Conclusion

As we leave this discussion, I want to return to what I said was the secret for your success in writing college essays: Your success with academic writing depends upon how well you understand what you are doing as you write and then how you approach the writing task. Hopefully, you now have a better idea about the nature of the academic writing task and the expectations behind it. Knowing what you need to do won't guarantee you an "A" on your paper—that will take a lot of thinking, hard work, and practice—but having the right orientation toward your college writing assignments is a first and important step in your eventual success.

Discussion

1. How did what you wrote in high school compare to what you have/will do in your academic writing in college?

2. Think of two different writing situations you have found yourself in. What did you need to do the same in those two situations to place your writing appropriately? What did you need to do differently?

3. Think of a writing assignment that you will need to complete this semester. Who's your audience? What's the occasion or context? What's your message? What's your purpose? What documents/genres are used? How does all that compare to the writing you are doing in this class?

Works Cited

Carroll, Lee Ann. *Rehearsing New Roles: How College Students Develop as Writers.* Carbondale: Southern Illinois UP, 2002. Print.

Thaiss, Chris and Terry Zawacki. *Engaged Writers & Dynamic Disciplines: Research on the Academic Writing Life.* Portsmouth: Boynton/Cook, 2006. Print.

Chapter
Two

Navigating Genres
by Kerry Dirk

There's a joke that's been floating around some time now that you've likely already heard. It goes something like the following:

Q: What do you get when you rewind a country song?

A: You get your wife back, your job back, your dog back...

Maybe this joke makes you laugh. Or groan. Or tilt your head to the side in confusion. Because it just so happens that in order to get this joke, you must know a little something about country music in general and in particular country music lyrics. You must, in other words, be familiar with the country music genre.

Let's look into country music lyrics a bit more. Bear with me on this is if you're not a fan. Assuming I want to write lyrics to a country song, how would I figure out what lyrics are acceptable in terms of country songs? Listening to any country station for a short period of time might leave one with the following conclusions about country songs:

- Country songs tend to tell stories. They often have characters who are developed throughout the song.

"Navgating Genres" by Kerry Dirk. *Writing Spaces: Readings on Writing*, Volume 1. Reprinted by permission of Kerry Dirk. http://writingspaces.org/sites/default/files/dirk--navigating-genres.pdf

- Country songs often have choruses that are broad enough to apply to a variety of verses.

- Country songs are often depressing; people lose jobs, lovers and friends.

- Country songs express pride for the country style and way of life.

- Country songs are often political, responding to wars and economic crises, for example.

Given these characteristics, I would feel prepared to write some new country lyrics. But what would happen if I wanted to write a country song that didn't do any of the above things? Would it still be a country song?

You are probably already familiar with many genres, although you may not know them as such; perhaps your knowledge of genres is limited to types of books, whether mystery, horror, action, etc. Now I'm going to ask you to stick with me while I show you how knowledge of genres goes far beyond a simple discussion of types. My purposes are to expand your definition of genre (or to introduce you to a definition for the first time) and to help you start thinking about how genres might apply to your own writing endeavors. But above all, I hope to give you an awareness of how genres function by taking what is often quite theoretical in the field of rhetoric and composition and making it a bit more tangible. So why was I talking about country songs? I think that using such references can help you to see, in a quite concrete way, how genres function.

When I started writing this essay, I had some ideas of what I wanted to say. But first, I had to determine what this essay might look like. I've written a lot—letters, nonfiction pieces, scholarly articles, rants—but this was my first time writing an essay to you, a composition student. What features, I asked myself, should go into this essay? How personal could I get? What rhetorical moves might I use, effectively or ineffectively? I hoped that a similar type of essay already existed so that I would have something to guide my own writing. I knew I was looking for other essays written directly to students, and after finding many examples, I looked for common features. In particular, I noted the warm, personal style that was prevalent through every essay; the tone was primarily conversational. And more importantly, I noticed that the writer did not talk as an authoritative figure but as a coach. Some writers admitted that they did not know everything (we don't), and others even went so far as to admit ignorance. I found myself doing what Mary Jo Reiff, a professor who studies rhetoric and composition, did when she was asked to write about her experience of writing an essay about teaching for those new to the field of composition. She writes, "I immediately called on my genre knowledge—my past experience with reading and writing similar texts in similar situations—to orient me to the expectations of this genre" (157).

I further acknowledged that it is quite rare that teachers of writing get to write so directly to students in such an informal manner. Although textbooks are directed at students, they are often more formal affairs meant to serve a different purpose than this essay. And because the genre of this essay is still developing, there are no formal expectations for what this paper might look like. In my excitement, I realized that perhaps I had been granted more freedom in writing this essay than is typical of an already established, although never static, genre. As a result, I decided to make this essay a mix of personal anecdotes, examples, and voices from teachers of writing. Such an essay seems to be the most fitting response to this situation, as I hope to come across as someone both informative and friendly. Why am I telling you this? Because it seems only appropriate that given the fact that I am talking about genre awareness, I should make you aware of my own struggles with writing in a new genre.

I will admit that the word genre used to have a bad reputation and may still make some people cringe. Genre used to refer primarily to form, which meant that writing in a particular genre was seen as simply a matter of filling in the blanks. Anne Freadman, a specialist in genre theory, points out that "it is this kind of genre theory with its failures that has caused the discredit of the very notion of genre, bringing about in turn its disuse and the disrepair many of us found it in" (46). But genre theory has come a long way since then. Perhaps the shift started when the rhetorician Lloyd Bitzer wrote the following:

> Due to either the nature of things or convention, or both, some situations recur. The courtroom is the locus for several kinds of situations generating the speech of accusation, the speech of defense, the charge to the jury. From day to day, year to year, comparable situations occur, prompting comparable responses; hence rhetorical forms are born and a special vocabulary, grammar, and style are established. (13)

In other words, Bitzer is saying that when something new happens that requires a response, someone must create that first response. Then when that situation happens again, another person uses the first response as a basis for the second, and eventually everyone who encounters this situation is basing his/her response on the previous ones, resulting in the creation of a new genre. Think about George Washington giving the first State of the Union Address. Because this genre was completely new, he had complete freedom to pick its form and content. All presidents following him now have these former addresses to help guide their response because the situation is now a reoccurring one. Amy Devitt, a professor who specializes in the study of genre theory, points out that "genres develop, then, because they respond appropriately to situations that writers encounter repeatedly" ("Generalizing" 576) and because "if each writing problem were to require a completely new assessment of how to respond, writing would be slowed considerably. But once we recognize a recurring situation, a situation that we or others have responded to in the past, our response to that situation can be guided by past responses" ("Generalizing"

576). As such, we can see how a genre like the State of the Union Address helps for more effective communication between the president and citizens because the president already has a genre with which to work; he/she doesn't have to create a new one, and citizens know what to expect from such an address.

The definition of genre has changed even more since Bitzer's article was written; genres are now viewed as even more than repeating rhetorical situations. Carolyn Miller, a leading professor in the field of technical communication, argues that "a rhetorically sound definition of genre must be centered…on the action it is used to accomplish" (151). How might this look? These actions don't have to be complex; many genres are a part of our daily lives. Think about genres as tools to help people to get things done. Devitt writes that:

> genres have the power to help or hurt human interaction, to ease communication or to deceive, to enable someone to speak or to discourage someone from saying something different. People learn how to do *small talk* to ease the social discomfort of large group gatherings and meeting new people, but advertisers learn how to disguise *sales letters as winning sweepstakes entries*. (*Writing* 1)

In other words, knowing what a genre is used for can help people to accomplish goals, whether that goal be getting a job by knowing how to write a stellar resume, winning a person's heart by writing a romantic love letter, or getting into college by writing an effective personal statement.

By this point you might realize that you have been participating in many different genres—whether you are telling a joke, writing an email, or uploading a witty status on Facebook. Because you know how these genres function as social actions, you can quite accurately predict how they function rhetorically; your joke should generate a laugh, your email should elicit a response, and your updated Facebook status should generate comments from your online friends. But you have done more than simply filled in the blanks. Possibly without even thinking about it, you were recognizing the rhetorical situation of your action and choosing to act in a manner that would result in the outcome you desired. I imagine that you would probably not share a risqué joke with your mom, send a "Hey Buddy" email to your professor, or update your Facebook status as "X has a huge wart on his foot." We can see that more than form matters here, as knowing what is appropriate in these situations obviously requires more rhetorical knowledge than does filling out a credit card form. Devitt argues that "people do not label a particular story as a joke solely because of formal features but rather because of their perception of the rhetorical action that is occurring" (*Writing* 11). True, genres often have formulaic features, but these features can change even as the nature of the genre remains (Devitt, *Writing*, 48). What is important to consider here is that if mastering a form were simply a matter of plugging in content, we would all be capable of successfully writing anything when we are given a formula. By now you likely know that writing is not that easy.

Fortunately, even if you have been taught to write in a formulaic way, you probably don't treat texts in such a manner. When approaching a genre for the first time, you likely view it as more than a simple form: "Picking up a text, readers not only classify it and expect a certain form, but also make assumptions about the text's purposes, its subject matter, its writer, and its expected reader" (Devitt, *Writing* 12). We treat texts that we encounter as rhetorical objects; we choose between horror movies and chick flicks not only because we are familiar with their forms but because we know what response they will elicit from us (nail-biting fear and dreamy sighs, respectively). Why am I picking popular genres to discuss? I think I agree with Miller when she argues the following:

> To consider as potential genres such homely discourse as the letter of recommendation, the user manual, the progress report, the ransom note, the lecture, and the white paper, as well as the eulogy, the apologia, the inaugural, the public proceeding, and the sermon, is not to trivialize the study of genres; it is to take seriously the rhetoric in which we are immersed and the situations in which we find ourselves. (155)

In other words, Miller is saying that all genres matter because they shape our everyday lives. And by studying the genres that we find familiar, we can start to see how specific choices that writers make result in specific actions on the part of readers; it only follows that our own writing must too be purposefully written.

I like examples, so here is one more. Many of you may be familiar with *The Onion*, a fictitious newspaper that uses real world examples to create humorous situations. Perhaps the most notable genre of *The Onion* is its headlines. The purpose of these headlines is simple: to make the reader respond by laughing. While many of the articles are also entertaining, the majority of the humor is produced through the headlines. In fact, the headlines are so important to the success of the newspaper that they are tested on volunteers to see the readers' immediate responses. There are no formal features of these headlines besides the fact that they are all quite brief; they share no specific style. But they are a rhetorical action meant to bring about a specific response, which is why I see them as being their own genre. A few examples for those of you unfamiliar with this newspaper would help to explain what I'm saying. Here are a few of my personal favorites (politically charged or other possibly offensive headlines purposefully avoided):

* "Archaeological Dig Uncovers Ancient Race of Skeleton People"
* "Don't Run Away, I'm Not the Flesh-Eating Kind of Zombie"
* "Time Traveler: Everyone In The Future Eats Dippin' Dots"
* "'I Am Under 18' Button Clicked For First Time In History Of Internet"

- "Commas, Turning Up, Everywhere"

- "Myspace Outage Leaves Millions Friendless"

- "Amazon.com Recommendations Understand Area Woman Better Than Husband"

- "Study: Dolphins Not So Intelligent On Land"

- "Beaver Overthinking Dam"

- "Study: Alligators Dangerous No Matter How Drunk You Are"

- "Child In Corner To Exact Revenge As Soon As He Gets Out" (*The Onion*)

I would surmise with near certainty that at least one of these headlines made you laugh. Why? I think the success lies in the fact that the writers of these headlines are rhetorically aware of whom these headlines are directed toward—college students like you, and more specifically, educated college students who know enough about politics, culture, and U.S. and world events to "get" these headlines.

And now for some bad news: figuring out a genre is tricky already, but this process is further complicated by the fact that two texts that might fit into the same genre might also look extremely different. But let's think about why this might be the case. Devitt points out, "different grocery stores make for different grocery lists. Different law courts make for different legal briefs. And different college classes make for different research papers. Location may not be the first, second, and third most important qualities of writing, as it is for real estate, but location is surely among the situational elements that lead to expected genres and to adaptations of those genres in particular situations" ("Transferability" 218). Think about a time when you were asked to write a research paper. You probably had an idea of what that paper should look like, but you also needed to consider the location of the assignment. In other words, you needed to consider how your particular teacher's expectations would help to shape your assignment. This makes knowing a genre about much more than simply knowing its form. You also need to consider the context in which it is being used. As such, it's important to be aware that the research paper you might be required to write in freshman composition might be completely different than the research paper you might be asked to write for an introductory psychology class. Your goal is to recognize these shifts in location and to be aware of how such shifts might affect your writing.

Let's consider a genre with which you are surely familiar: the thesis statement. Stop for a moment and consider what this term means to you. Ask your classmates. It's likely that you each have your own definition of what a thesis statement should and should not look like. You may have heard never to start a thesis statement with a phrase like "In this essay." Or you might have been taught that a thesis statement should have three parts, each of which will be discussed in one paragraph of the essay. I learned that many good thesis statements follow the formula "X because Y," where "X" refers to a specific stance, and "Y" refers to a specific reason for taking that stance. For example, I could argue "School uniforms should be required because they will help students to focus more on academics and less on fashion." Now, whether or not this is a good thesis statement is irrelevant, but you can see how following the "X because Y" formula would produce a nicely structured statement. Take this a step further and research "thesis statements" on the Internet, and you'll find that there are endless suggestions. And despite their vast differences, they all fit under the genre of thesis statement. How is this possible? Because it comes back to the particular situation in which that thesis statement is being used. Again, location is everything.

I think it's time to try our hand at approaching a genre with which I hope all of you are only vaguely familiar and completely unpracticed: the ransom note.

A Scenario

I've decided to kidnap Bob's daughter Susie for ransom. I'm behind on the mortgage payments, my yacht payments are also overdue, and I desperately need money. It is well known that Bob is one of the wealthiest people in Cash City, so I've targeted him as my future source of money. I've never met Bob, although one time his Mercedes cut me off in traffic, causing me to hit the brakes and spill my drink; the stain still glares at me from the floor of the car. The kidnapping part has been completed; now I need to leave Bob a ransom note. Let's look at a few drafts I've completed to decide which one would be most appropriate.

Ransom Letter 1:

> If you ever want to see your daughter alive again, leave 1 million dollars by the blue garbage can at 123 Ransom Rd. at Midnight. Come alone and do not call the police.

Ransom Letter 2:

> Hav daughter. Million $. Blu grbg can 123 Ransom Rd. 12AM. No poliz.

Ransom Letter 3:

> Dear Bob,
>
> Thank you for taking the time to read this letter. You have a lovely house, and I very much enjoyed my recent visit while you were out of town. Unfortunately, I have kidnapped your daughter. As I am currently unable to meet several financial demands, I am graciously turning to you for help in this matter. I am sure that we will be able to come to some mutually beneficial agreement that results in the return

of your daughter and the padding of my wallet. Please meet with me at the Grounds Coffee House on First Street so that we may discuss what price is most fitting. Your daughter, meanwhile, remains in safe and competent hands. She is presently playing pool with my son Matt (a possible love connection?), and she says to tell you "Hi."

Yours truly, Jim

P.S. Please order me a skim vanilla latte, should you arrive before I do.

Immediately, you can probably determine that ransom letter one is the best choice. But have you considered why? What does the first letter have that the other two are lacking? Let's first eliminate the most obvious dud—letter number three. Not only does it mimic the friendly, familiar manner of two friends rather than the threatening note of a deranged kidnapper, but it also suggests both that there is no rush in the matter and that the price is negotiable. Letters one and two are closer; they both contain the same information, but letter two fails to be as rhetorically strong as number one. The spelling errors and choppy feel might suggest that the writer of the note is not intelligent enough to get away with the kidnapping. The first letter is the most rhetorically strong because it is well written and direct. All of these letters would qualify as fitting the genre of ransom letter, but the first one most obviously fits the rhetorical situation.

It may be worthwhile to note some particular challenges you might have to approaching your writing genres as rhetorical situations. Perhaps you have come from a writing background where you learned that certain rules apply to all writing. Just nod if these sound familiar:

* You must have a thesis statement at the end of the introduction.

* Every thesis statement should introduce three points of discussion.

* You cannot use "I" in writing.

* You cannot begin a sentence with a coordinating conjunction.

* Every paragraph should start with a topic sentence.

You get the point. These rules are appealing; they tell us exactly what to do and not to do with regard to writing. I remember happily creating introductions that moved from broad to specific (often starting with "In our world"), constructing three point thesis statements, and beginning paragraphs with "first," "second," and "third." I didn't have to think about audience, or purpose, or even much about content for that matter. All that really mattered was that essay followed a certain formula that was called good writing. But looking back, what resulted from such formulas was not very good; actually, it was quite bad.

That is, of course, not to say that there aren't rules that come with genres; the difference is that the rules change as the genre changes, that no rules apply to all genres, and that genres require more effort than simply following the rules. Because genres usually come with established conventions, it is risky to choose not to follow such conventions. These similarities within genres help us to communicate successfully; imagine the chaos that would ensue if news broadcasts were done in raps, if all legal briefs were written in couplets, or if your teacher handed you a syllabus and told you that it must first be decoded. In sum, "too much choice is as debilitating of meaning as is too little choice. In language, too much variation results eventually in lack of meaning: mutual unintelligibility" (Devitt, "Genre" 53).

But on a brighter note, genres also help us to make more efficient decisions when writing, as we can see how people have approached similar situations. Creating a new genre each time that writing was required would make the writing process much longer, as we would not have past responses to help us with present ones (Devitt, "Generalizing" 576). As a result, the more you are able to master particular genres, the better equipped you may be to master genres that you later encounter:

> When people write, they draw on the genres they know, their own context of genres, to help construct their rhetorical action. If they encounter a situation new to them, it is the genres they have acquired in the past that they can use to shape their new action. Every genre they acquire, then, expands their genre repertoire and simultaneously shapes how they might view new situations. (Devitt, *Writing* 203)

Taking what Devitt says into account, think back to the previous discussion of the research paper. If you already have some idea of what a research paper looks like, you do not have to learn an entirely new genre. Instead, you just have to figure out how to change that particular genre to fit with the situation, even if that change just comes from having a different teacher.

Learning about genres and how they function is more important than mastering one particular genre; it is this knowledge that helps us to recognize and to determine appropriate responses to different situations—that is, knowing what particular genre is called for in a particular situation. And learning every genre would be impossible anyway, as Devitt notes that "no writing class could possibly teach students all the genres they will need to succeed even in school, much less in the workplace or in their civic lives. Hence the value of teaching genre awareness rather than acquisition of particular genres" (*Writing* 205). This approach helps to make you a more effective writer as well, as knowing about genres will make you more prepared to use genres that you won't learn in college. For example, I recently needed to write a letter about removing a late fee on a credit card. I had never written this particular type of letter before, but I knew what action I was trying to accomplish. As a result, I did some research on writing letters and determined that I should make it as formal and polite as possible. The body of the letter ended up as follows:

> I have very much enjoyed being a card carrier with this bank for many years. However, I recently had a late fee charged to my account. As you will note from my previous statements, this is the first late fee I have ever acquired. I do remember making this payment on time, as I have all of my previous payments. I hope to remain a loyal customer of this bank for many years to come, so I would very much appreciate it if you would remove this charge from my account.

You can see that this letter does several things. First, I build credibility for myself by reminding them that I have used their card for many years. Second, I ask them to check my records to show further that I am typically a responsible card carrier. And third, I hint that if they do not remove the late fee, I might decide to change to a different bank. This letter is effective because it considers how the situation affects the genre. And yes, the late fee was removed.

Chances are that I have left you more confused than you were before you began this essay. Actually, I hope that I have left you frustrated; this means that the next time you write, you will have to consider not only form but also audience, purpose, and genre; you will, in other words, have to consider the rhetorical effectiveness of your writing. Luckily, I can leave you with a few suggestions:

- First, determine what action you are trying to accomplish. Are you trying to receive an A on a paper? Convince a credit card company to remove a late fee? Get into graduate school? If you don't know what your goal is for a particular writing situation, you'll have a difficult time figuring out what genre to use.

- Second, learn as much as you can about the situation for which you are writing. What is the purpose? Who is the audience? How much freedom do you have? How does the location affect the genre?

- Third, research how others have responded to similar situations. Talk to people who have written what you are trying to write. If you are asked to write a biology research paper, ask your instructor for examples. If you need to write a cover letter for a summer internship, take the time to find out about the location of that internship.

- And finally, ask questions.

Discussion

1. What are some genres that you feel you know well? How did you learn them? What are their common rhetorical features?

2. What rules have you been told to follow in the past? How did they shape what you were writing?

3. How much freedom do you enjoy when writing? Does it help to have a form to follow, or do you find it to be limiting?

Works Cited

Bitzer, Lloyd F. "The Rhetorical Situation." *Philosophy and Rhetoric* 1.1 (1968): 1–14. Print.

Devitt, Amy J. "Generalizing About Genre: New Conceptions of an Old Concept." *College Composition and Communication* 44.4 (1993): 573–86. Print.

—. "Genre as Language Standard." *Genre and Writing: Issues, Arguments, Alternatives.* Ed. Wendy Bishop and Hans Ostrom. Portsmouth, NH: Boynton/Cook, 1997. 45–55. Print.

—. "Transferability and Genres." *The Locations of Composition.* Ed. Christopher J. Keller and Christian R. Weisser. Albany, NY: SUNY P, 2007. 215–27. Print.

—. *Writing Genres.* Carbondale: Southern Illinois UP, 2004. Print.

Freadman, Anne. "Anyone for Tennis." *Genre and the New Rhetoric.* Ed. Aviva Freedman and Peter Medway. Bristol: Taylor & Francis, 1994. 43–66. Print.

Miller, Carolyn R. "Genre as Social Action." *Quarterly Journal of Speech* 70.2 (1984): 151–67. Print.

The Onion: America's Finest News Source. 20 July 2009. Web. 20 July 2009. <http://www.theonion.com>.

Reiff, Mary Jo. "Moving Writers, Shaping Motives, Motivating Critique and Change: A Genre Approach to Teaching Writing." *Relations, Locations, Positions: Composition Theory for Writing Teachers.* Ed. Peter Vandenberg, Sue Hum, and Jennifer Clary-Lemon. Urbana, IL: National Council of Teachers of English, 2006. 157–64. Print.

Questions to Ask About Your Own Projects

- What is my purpose for writing?
  - Am I writing mainly for reader understanding? Do I want to change their views?
  - Do I want the audience to take a specific action?
  - Do I want to build a relationship with the audience?
  - Have I seen any models of the assignment I've been asked to write? What can those models show me about success and/or challenges with this genre?
- What are the features or characteristics of the genre I'm working with?
- What are the things the genre will allow me to and/or stop me from doing?
  - What kind of style can I write in?
  - What kind of tone can I use?
  - What kind of role or persona am I taking on as the writer?
  - What do I want to do or say that doesn't seem to fit into this genre? How might I adapt or "push the envelope" to meet my needs?
- How will writing in this genre be affected by the situation in which I'm writing?
  - How does the discipline of the class (humanities, natural sciences, applied sciences, social sciences) shape the assignment?
  - What specific instructions has my teacher provided?
- Thinking about what I want to do and what the assignment asks me to do, what questions do I have for my teacher?
- Have I made a plan for drafting my assignment?
  - Did I plan time for completing my first draft and then revising (multiple times)?
  - Do I know my strengths and challenges as an individual writer?
  - Should I make one or more appointments with the Writing Center for additional support through the drafting process?
  - What are my instructor's office hours, so I can drop by with questions or drafts?

Section Two

Reading and Writing as Integrated Processes

The two readings in this section lend a bird's-eye view of the reading and writing strategies used in university classes. Reading and writing are integrated activities: to prepare for writing, you usually need to read first, and your practice reading will help you become a better writer. As you consider "Reading Processes" by Kennedy, Kennedy, and Muth, think about your own strategies for working through a long or challenging document. As you read "A Writer's Choices," realize it is a summary of everything that happens from the beginning to the end of an assignment. The writing process is introduced in a concise way so you get an overview of the whole thing. Then, throughout the semester, we'll return to and study in more depth various parts of this process. Questions that follow the readings should remind you of the key points.

Chapter Three

Reading Processes

by X. J. Kennedy, Dorothy M. Kennedy, and Marcia F. Muth

What's so special about college reading? Don't you pick up the book, start on the first page, and keep going, just as you have ever since you met *The Cat in the Hat*? Reading from beginning to end works especially well when you are eager to find out what happens next, as in a thriller, or what to do next, as in a cookbook. On the other hand, much of what you read in college—textbooks, scholarly articles, research reports, your peers' papers—is complicated and challenging. Dense material like this often requires closer reading and deeper thinking—in short, a process for reading critically.

Reading critically is a useful skill. For assignments in this course alone, you probably will need to evaluate the strengths and weaknesses of essays by professionals and students. If you research any topic, you will need to figure out what your sources say, whether they are reliable, and how you might use their information. Critical reading is important in other courses too. For example, you might analyze a sociology report on violent children for its assumptions and implications as well as the soundness of its argument. When your writing relies on critical reading, you generally need to explain what is going on in the reading material and then go further, making your own point based on what you have read.

A Process of Critical Reading

Reading critically means approaching whatever you read in an active, questioning manner. This essential college-level skill changes reading from a spectator sport to a contact sport. You no longer sit in the stands, watching figure skaters glide by. Instead, you charge right into a rough-and-tumble hockey game, gripping your stick and watching out for your teeth.

Critical reading, like critical thinking, is not an isolated activity. It is a continuum of strategies that thoughtful people use every day to grapple with new information, to integrate it with existing knowledge, and to apply it to problems in daily life and in academic courses. Many readers use similar strategies:

- They get ready to do their reading.

- They respond as they read.

- They read on literal and analytical levels.

Preparing to Read

College reading is active reading. Before you read, think ahead about how to approach the reading process, how to make the most of the time you spend reading.

Thinking about Your Purpose. Naturally, your overall goal for doing most college reading is to succeed in your courses. When you begin to read, ask questions like these about your immediate purpose:

- What are you reading?

- Why are you reading?

- What do you want to do with the reading?

- What does your instructor expect you to learn from the reading?

- Do you need to memorize details, find main points, or connect ideas?

- How does this reading build on, add to, contrast with, or otherwise relate to other reading assignments in the course?

Planning Your Follow-up. When you are assigned a specific essay, chapter, or article or are required to choose a reading about a certain topic, ask yourself what your instructor probably expects to follow the reading:

- Do you need to be ready to discuss the reading during class?

- Will you need to mention it or analyze it during an examination?

- Will you need to write about it or its topic?

- Do you need to find its main points? Sum it up? Compare it? Question it? Discuss its strengths and weaknesses? Draw useful details from it?

Skimming the Text. Before you actively read a text, begin by skimming it, quickly reading only enough to introduce yourself to its content and organization. If the reading has a table of contents or subheadings, read those first to figure out what the material covers and how it is organized. Read the first paragraph and then the first (or first and last) sentence of each paragraph that follows. If the material has any illustrations or diagrams, read the captions.

Responding to Reading

Encourage yourself to read energetically by monitoring both what you read and how you respond to it.

Reading Deeply. The books and articles assigned in college often require more concentration from you as a reader than simpler readings do. Use the following questions to help you understand the complexities below the surface of a reading:

- Are difficult or technical terms defined in specific ways? How might you highlight, list, or record those terms so that you can master them?

- How might you record or recall the details in the reading? How might you track or diagram interrelated ideas to grasp the connections?

- How does word choice, tone, or style alert you to the complex purpose of a reading that is layered or indirect rather than straightforward?

- How might you trace the progression of ideas in the reading? Where do you spot headings, previews of what's coming up, summaries of what's gone before, transitions, and other clues to the reading's organization?

- Does the reading include figurative or descriptive language, allusions to other works, or recurring themes? How do these elements enrich the reading?

Keeping a Reading Journal. A reading journal helps you read actively and build a reservoir of ideas for follow-up writing. You can use a special notebook or computer file to address questions like these:

- What is the subject of the reading? What is the writer's stand?

- What does the writer take for granted? What assumptions does he or she begin with? Where are these assumptions stated or suggested?

- What evidence supports the writer's main points?

- Do you agree with what the writer is saying? Do his or her ideas clash with your ideas or call into question something you take for granted?

- Has the writer taken account of other views, opinions, or interpretations of evidence?

- What conclusions can you draw from the reading?

- Has the reading opened your eyes to new ways of viewing the subject?

Annotating the Text. Writing notes on the page (or on a photocopy if the material is not your own) is a useful way to trace the author's points and to respond to them with questions or comments. You can underline key points, mark checks and stars by ideas when you agree or disagree, and jot questions in the margins. (A Critical Reading Checklist appears later in this chapter.) When one student investigated the history of women's professional sports, she annotated a key passage from an article called "Why Men Fear Women's Teams" by Kate Rounds from the January–February 1991 issue of *Ms.*

Different case from individual sports

Key point

By contrast, women's professional (team) sports have failed spectacularly. Since the mid-seventies, every

bitter tone

professional league—softball, basketball, and volleyball—has gone belly-up. In 1981, after a four-year struggle, the Women's Basketball League (WBL), backed by sports promoter Bill Byrne, folded. The

✓

First example backs up point

What women's teams have gotten these?

league was drawing fans in a number of cities, but the sponsors weren't there, TV wasn't there, and nobody seemed to miss the spectacle of a few good women fighting for a basketball.

✓

Something I know about!

Why does she call it this?

Or a (volleyball) for that matter. Despite the success of (bikini) volleyball, an organization called MLV (Major League Volleyball) bit the dust in March of 1989 after nearly three years of struggling for sponsorship, fan support, and television exposure. [As with pro basketball, there was a man behind women's professional volleyball,] real estate investor Robert (Bat) Batinovich. Batinovich admits that, unlike court volleyball, beach volleyball has a lot of "visual T&A mixed into it."

Second example

What court volleyball does have, according to former MLV executive director Lindy Vivas, is strong women athletes. Vivas is assistant volleyball coach at San Jose State University. "The United States in general," she says, "has problems dealing with women athletes and strong, aggressive females. The perception is you have to be more aggressive in team sports than in golf and tennis, which aren't contact sports. Women athletes are looked at as masculine and get the stigma of being gay."

This student's annotations helped her deepen her reading of the article and generate ideas for her writing.

A Spotlight on Reading Levels

Educational expert Benjamin Bloom identified six levels of cognitive activity: knowledge, comprehension, application, analysis, synthesis, and evaluation.* Each level acts as a foundation for the next. Each also becomes more complex and demands higher thinking skills than the previous one. (See Figure 1.) Experienced readers, however, may jump among these levels, gathering information and insight as they occur.

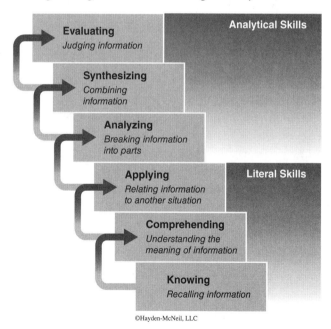

©Hayden-McNeil, LLC

Figure 1. Using Literal and Analytical Reading Skills. SOURCE: The information in this figure is adapted from Benjamin S. Bloom et al., *Taxonomy of Educational Objectives, Handbook 1: Cognitive Domain* (New York: McKay, 1956).

---

*   Benjamin S. Bloom et al., *Taxonomy of Educational Objectives, Handbook 1: Cognitive Domain*. Copyright © 1956 by David McKay, Inc.

The first three levels are literal skills. When you show that you know a fact, comprehend its meaning, and can apply it to a new situation, you demonstrate your mastery over building blocks of thought. The last three levels—analysis, synthesis, and evaluation—are critical skills. These skills take you beyond the literal level: you break apart the building blocks to see what makes them work, recombine them in new and useful ways, and judge their worth or significance. To read critically, you must engage with a piece on both literal and analytical levels.

Reading on Literal Levels

As you first tackle an unfamiliar reading, you may struggle simply to discover what—exactly—it presents to readers. When you read literally, you decode the words in the passage, figure out the meaning, and connect the information to what you already know. For example, suppose you read in your history book a passage about Franklin Delano Roosevelt (FDR), the only American president elected to four consecutive terms of office.

Becoming Aware of the Information. Once you read the passage, even if you have little background in American history, you know and can recall the information it presents about FDR and his four terms in office.

Comprehending the Information. To comprehend the information, you need to know that a term for a U.S. president is four years and that *consecutive* means "continuous." Thus, FDR was elected to serve for sixteen years.

Applying the Information. To apply this knowledge, you think of other presidents—George Washington, who served two terms; Grover Cleveland, who served two terms but not consecutively; Jimmy Carter, who served one term; and Bill Clinton, who served two terms. Then you realize that being elected to four terms is unusual. In fact, the Twenty-Second Amendment to the Constitution, ratified in 1951, now limits a president to two terms.

Reading on Analytical Levels

After mastering a passage on the literal levels, you need to read on the analytical levels, probing the meaning beneath the surface. First, you analyze the information, considering its parts and implications from various angles. Then you gather related material and synthesize all of it, combining it to achieve new insights. Finally, you evaluate the significance of the information.

Analyzing the Information. To return to FDR's four terms as president, you can ask questions to scrutinize this information from various angles, selecting a principle that suits your purpose to break the information into its components or parts. For example, you might analyze FDR's tenure in office in relation to the political longevity of other presidents. Why has FDR been the only president elected to serve four terms? What circumstances during his terms contributed to three reelections? How is FDR different from other presidents?

Synthesizing the Information. To answer your questions, you may have to read more or review material you have read in the past. Then you begin synthesizing—combining information, pulling together the facts and opinions, identifying the evidence accepted by all or most sources, examining any controversial evidence, and drawing whatever conclusions reliable evidence seems to support. For example, it would be logical to conclude that the special circumstances of the Great Depression and World War II contributed to FDR's four terms. On the other hand, it would not be logical to conclude that Americans reelected FDR out of pity because he was a victim of polio.

Evaluating the Information. Finally, you evaluate your new knowledge to determine its significance, both to your understanding of Depression-era politics and to your assessment of your history book's approach. For instance, you might ask yourself why the book's author has chosen to make this point. How does it affect the rest of the discussion? Does this author seem reliable? And you may also have formed your own opinion about FDR's reelections, perhaps concluding that FDR's four-term presidency is understandable in light of the events of the 1930s and 1940s, that the author has mentioned this fact to highlight the unique political atmosphere of that era, and that, in your opinion, it is evidence neither for nor against FDR's excellence as a president.

Generating Ideas from Reading

Like flints that strike each other and cause sparks, writers and readers provoke one another. For example, when your class discusses an essay, you may be surprised by the range of insights your classmates report. If you missed some of their insights during your reading, remember that they may be equally surprised by what you see.

Often you look to other writers—in books or articles—to suggest a topic, provide information about it, or help you explain it or back it up with evidence. You may read because you want to understand ideas, test them, or debate with the writer, but reading is a dynamic process. You may find that it changes your ideas instead of supporting them. Here are suggestions for unlocking the potential hidden in a good text.

Looking for Meaty Pieces. Stimulate your thinking about current topics that intrigue you by browsing through essay collections or magazines in the library or online. Try *The Atlantic, Harper's, The New Republic, Commentary,* or a special-interest magazine like *Architectural Digest* or *Scientific American.* Check the editorials and op-ed columns in your local newspaper, the *New York Times*, or the *Wall Street Journal*. Also search the Internet on interesting subjects that challenge you to think seriously (for example, film classics or the effects of poverty on children). Look for articles that are meaty, not super-ficial, and that are written to inform and convince, not to entertain or amuse.

Logging Your Reading. For several days keep a log of the articles that you find. Record the author, title, and source for each promising piece so that you can easily find it again. Briefly note the subject and point of view in order to identify a range of possibilities.

Recalling Something You Have Already Read. What have you read lately that started you thinking? Return to a recent reading—a chapter in a humanities textbook, an article assigned in a sociology course, a research study for a biology course.

Capturing Complex Ideas. When you find a challenging reading, do you sometimes feel too overwhelmed to develop ideas from it? If so, read it slowly and carefully. Then consider two common methods of recording and integrating ideas from sources into papers. First, try *paraphrasing*, restating the author's ideas fully but in your own words. Then try *summarizing*, reducing the author's main point to essentials. Accurately restat-ing what a reading says can help you grasp its ideas, especially on literal levels. Once you understand what it says, you are better equipped to agree with, disagree with, or question its points.

Reading Critically. Read first literally and then analytically. Instead of just soaking up what the reading says, engage in a dialogue or conversation with the writer. Criticize. Wonder. Argue back. Demand convincing evidence. Use the following checklist to get you started as a critical reader.

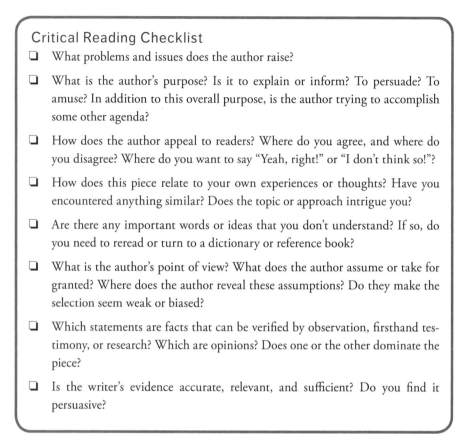

Critical Reading Checklist

❑ What problems and issues does the author raise?

❑ What is the author's purpose? Is it to explain or inform? To persuade? To amuse? In addition to this overall purpose, is the author trying to accomplish some other agenda?

❑ How does the author appeal to readers? Where do you agree, and where do you disagree? Where do you want to say "Yeah, right!" or "I don't think so!"?

❑ How does this piece relate to your own experiences or thoughts? Have you encountered anything similar? Does the topic or approach intrigue you?

❑ Are there any important words or ideas that you don't understand? If so, do you need to reread or turn to a dictionary or reference book?

❑ What is the author's point of view? What does the author assume or take for granted? Where does the author reveal these assumptions? Do they make the selection seem weak or biased?

❑ Which statements are facts that can be verified by observation, firsthand testimony, or research? Which are opinions? Does one or the other dominate the piece?

❑ Is the writer's evidence accurate, relevant, and sufficient? Do you find it persuasive?

Analyzing Writing Strategies. Reading widely and deeply can reveal not only what others say but also how they say it and how they shape such key features as the introduction, thesis statement or main idea, major points, and supporting evidence. Ask questions like those in the following Writing Strategies Checklist to help you identify writing strategies.

Writing Strategies Checklist

❏   How does the author introduce the reading? In what ways does the author try to engage readers?

❏   Where does the author state or imply the main idea or thesis?

❏   How is the text organized? What are the main points used to develop the thesis? What does the selection of these points suggest about the author's approach?

❏   How does the author supply support—facts, data, statistics, expert opinions, personal experiences, observations, explanations, examples, or other information?

❏   How does the author connect or emphasize ideas for readers?

❏   How does the author conclude the reading?

❏   What is the author's tone? How do the words and examples reveal the author's attitude, biases, or assumptions?

Chapter Four

A Writer's Choices:
An Overview of the Writing Process
by Andrea A. Lunsford

You send a text message to your friend confirming weekend plans. Later on, you put together an analysis of cost-cutting possibilities for the manager of the company you're interning for. And later still, you pull out the notes you took on your biology experiment and write up the lab report that is due tomorrow. In between, you probably do a lot of other writing as well—notes, lists, blog entries, Facebook status updates, and so on.

These are the kinds of writing most of us do every day, more or less easily, yet each demands that we make important choices. In your text message, you probably use a kind of shorthand, not bothering to write complete sentences or even entire words. For your boss, however, you probably choose to be more formal and "correct." And for your lab report, you probably choose to follow the format your instructor requires. In each case, the choices you make as a writer are based on your **rhetorical situation**—the entire context for the writing.

Moving Between Social and Academic Writing

Students are doing more writing and reading today than ever before, and much of it is online—on Facebook, Twitter, Tumblr, and other social media sites. Writing on social networking sites allows almost instant feedback; anticipating audience responses can make online writers very savvy about analyzing audiences and about using an appropriate style and tone for the occasion.

Student Stephanie Parker tweeted:

> Rain's over, going to Trader Joe's for some healthy stuff to fight this cold ... suggestions?

Student Erin McLaughlin posted on Facebook:

> Help send one of my Ghanian friends to college. The smallest contribution helps!
> http://www.indiegogo.com/teachaman

In these two short messages, Stephanie and Erin show a keen awareness of audience and two common purposes for social writing—to ask for information (healthy food suggestions for Stephanie) and to give information (about a cause Erin supports). Erin is asking her audience to help a friend from Ghana go to college, and since most of her friends are also college students, she assures them that they don't need to have a lot of money to make a difference.

Like Stephanie and Erin, you are probably adept at informal social writing across a range of genres and media. You may not think very hard about your audience for a tweet or Facebook post, or about your purpose for writing in such spaces, but you are probably more skilled than you give yourself credit for when it comes to making appropriate choices for informal writing.

In the writing you do from now on, you'll need to be able to move back and forth between informal and formal situations. Look closely at your informal writing: What do you assume about your audience? What is your purpose? How do you represent yourself online? What do the photos you post and your likes and dislikes say about you? Analyzing the choices you make in an informal writing context will help you develop the ability to make good choices in other contexts as well.

Meeting Expectations for Academic Writing

Expectations about academic writing vary considerably from field to field, but becoming familiar with widespread conventions will prepare you well for writing in most academic contexts.

Authority

Most instructors expect you to begin to establish your own authority—to become a constructive critic who can analyze and interpret the works of others.

To establish authority, assume that your opinions count and that your audience expects you to present them in a well-reasoned manner. Show your familiarity with the ideas and works of others, both from the assigned course reading and from good points your instructor and classmates have made.

Directness and Clarity

Good academic writing prepares readers for what is coming next, provides definitions, and includes topic sentences.

To achieve directness in your writing, try the following strategies:

- State your main point early and clearly.

- Avoid overqualifying your statements. Instead of writing *I think the facts reveal,* come right out and say *The facts reveal.*

- Avoid digressions. If you use an anecdote or example from personal experience, be sure it relates directly to the point you are making.

- Use appropriate evidence, such as examples and concrete details, to support each point.

- Make obvious and clear transitions from point to point.

- Follow logical organizational patterns.

- Design and format the project appropriately for the audience and purpose you have in mind.

Considering the Assignment and Purpose; Choosing a Topic

For the writing you do that isn't connected to a class or work assignment, you may have a clear purpose in mind. Even so, analyzing exactly what you want to accomplish and why can help you communicate more effectively.

An academic assignment may explain why, for whom, and about what you are supposed to write, or it may seem to come out of the blue. Make an effort to understand what your instructor expects.

*   What is the primary purpose of your writing—to persuade? to explain? to entertain? something else?

*   What purpose did the person who gave you the assignment want to achieve—to test your understanding? to evaluate your writing abilities? to encourage you to think outside the box?

*   What, exactly, does the assignment ask you to do? Look for words such as *analyze*, *explain*, *prove*, and *survey*.

If you have the opportunity to choose your own topic, look to topics that compel, puzzle, or pose a problem for you; these are likely to engage your interests and hence produce your best writing.

*   Can you focus the topic enough to write about it effectively in the time and space available?

*   What do you know about the topic? What else do you need to learn?

*   What seems most important about it?

*   What do you expect to conclude about the topic? (Remember, you may change your mind.)

Reaching Appropriate Audiences

Every communicator can benefit from thinking carefully about who the audience is, what the audience already knows or thinks, and what the audience needs and expects to find out. One of the characteristics of an effective communicator is the ability to write for a variety of audiences, using language, style, and evidence appropriate to particular readers, listeners, or viewers.

*   What audience do you want to reach—people who are already sympathetic to your views? people who disagree with you? members of a group you belong to? members of a group you don't belong to?

- In what ways are the members of your audience different from you? from one another?

- What assumptions can you make about your audience? What might they value— brevity, originality, honesty, wit? How can you appeal to their values?

- What sorts of evidence will your audience find most compelling—quotations from experts? personal experiences? statistics? images?

- What responses do you want as a result of what you write?

Considering Stance and Tone

Knowing your own stance—where you are coming from—can help you think about ways to get your readers to understand and perhaps share your views. What is your overall attitude toward the topic—approval? disapproval? curiosity? What social, political, religious, or other factors account for your attitude? You should also be aware of any preconceptions about your topic that may affect your stance.

Your purpose, audience, and stance will help to determine the tone your writing should take. Should it be humorous? serious? impassioned? Think about ways to show that you are knowledgeable and trustworthy. Remember, too, that visual and audio elements can influence the tone of your writing as much as the words you choose.

Considering Time, Genre, Medium, and Format

Many other elements of your context for a particular writing project will shape the final outcome.

- How much time will you have for the project? Do you need to do research or learn unfamiliar technology? Allow time for revision and editing.

- What genre does your text call for—a review? an argument essay? a lab report? a blog post? Study examples if you are unfamiliar with the genre.

- In what medium will the text appear—on the open Internet? on a password-protected site? in a print essay? in a presentation? Will you use images, video, or audio?

- What kind of organization should you use?

- How will you document your sources? Will your audience expect a particular documentation style?

Collaborating

Writers often work together to come up with ideas, to respond to one another's drafts, or even to coauthor texts. Here are some strategies for working with others:

- Establish ground rules for the collaboration. Be sure every writer has an equal opportunity—and responsibility—to contribute.

- Exchange contact information, and plan face-to-face meetings (if any).

- Pay close attention to each writer's views. Expect disagreement, and remember that the goal is to talk through all possibilities.

- If you are preparing a collaborative document, divide up the drafting duties and set reasonable deadlines.

- In team projects, acknowledge all members' contributions as well as any help you receive from outsiders.

Exploring a Topic

Among the most important parts of the writing process are choosing a topic, exploring what you know about it, and determining what you need to find out. The following strategies can help you explore your topic:

- Brainstorm. Try out ideas. Jot down key words about the topic, and see what they prompt you to think about next.

- Freewrite without stopping for ten minutes or so to see what insights or ideas you come up with.

- Draw or make word pictures about your topic.

- Try clustering—writing your topic on a sheet of paper, then writing related thoughts near the topic idea. Draw lines to show how ideas are connected.

- Ask questions about the topic: *What is it? What caused it? What larger system is the topic a part of? What do people say about it?* Or choose the journalist's questions: *Who? What? When? Where? Why? How?*

- Browse sources to find out what others say about the topic.

Developing a Working Thesis

Academic and professional writing in the United States often contains an explicit **thesis statement**. You should establish a working thesis early in your writing process. Your final thesis may be very different from the working thesis you begin with. Even so, a working thesis focuses your thinking and research, and helps keeps you on track.

A working thesis should have two parts: a topic, which indicates the subject matter the writing is about, and a comment, which makes an important point about the topic.

▶ **In the graphic novel *Fun Home*, images and words combine to make meanings that are more subtle than either words alone or images alone could convey.**

A successful working thesis has three characteristics:

1. It is potentially *interesting* to the intended audience.

2. It is as specific as possible.

3. It limits the topic enough to make it *manageable*.

You can evaluate a working thesis by checking it against each of these characteristics, as in the following examples:

▶ **Graphic novels combine words and images.**

INTERESTING?   The topic of graphic novels could be interesting, but this draft of a working thesis has no real comment attached to it—instead, it states a bare fact, and the only place to go from here is to more bare facts.

▶ **In graphic novels, words and images convey interesting meanings.**

SPECIFIC?   This thesis is not specific. What are "interesting meanings," exactly? How are they conveyed?

▶ **Graphic novels have evolved in recent decades to become an important literary genre.**

MANAGEABLE?   This thesis would not be manageable for a short-term project because it would require research on several decades of history and on hundreds of texts from all over the world.

Gathering Evidence and Doing Research

What kinds of evidence will be most persuasive to your audience and most effective in the field you are working in—historical precedents? expert testimony? statistical data? experimental results? personal anecdotes? Knowing what kinds of evidence count most in a particular field or with particular audiences will help you make appropriate choices.

If the evidence you need calls for research, determine what research you need to do:

• Make a list of what you already know about your topic.

• Keep track of where information comes from so you can return to your sources later.

• What else do you need to know, and where are you likely to find good sources of information?

Planning and Drafting

Sketch out a rough plan for organizing your writing. You can simply begin with your thesis; review your notes, research materials, and media; and list all the evidence you have to support the thesis. An informal way to organize your ideas is to figure out what belongs in your introduction, body paragraphs, and conclusion. You may also want—or be required—to make a formal outline, which can help you see exactly how the parts of your writing fit together.

The technique of storyboarding—working out a narrative or argument in visual form—can also be a good way to come up with an organizational plan. You can create your own storyboard by using note cards or sticky notes, taking advantage of different colors to keep track of threads of argument, subtopics, and so on. Move the cards and notes around, trying out different arrangements, until you find an organization that works well for your writing situation.

Checklist: Drafting

❏ **Set up a folder or file for your essay.** Give the file a clear and relevant name, and save to it often. Number your drafts. If you decide to try a new direction, save the file as a new draft.

❏ **Have all your information close at hand and arranged according to your organizational plan.** Stopping to search for a piece of information can break your concentration or distract you.

❏ **Try to write in stretches of at least thirty minutes.** Writing can provide momentum, and once you get going, the task becomes easier.

❏ **Don't let small questions bog you down.** Just make a note of them in brackets—or in all caps—or make a tentative decision and move on.

❏ **Remember that first drafts aren't perfect.** Concentrate on getting your ideas down, and don't worry about anything else.

Developing Paragraphs

The three qualities essential to most academic paragraphs are unity, development, and coherence.

Unity

An effective paragraph focuses on one main idea. You can achieve unity by stating the main idea clearly in one sentence—the topic sentence—and relating all other sentences in the paragraph to that idea. Like a thesis, the topic sentence includes a topic and a comment on that topic. A topic sentence often begins a paragraph, but it may come at the end—or be implied rather than stated directly.

Development

In addition to being unified, a paragraph should hold readers' interest and explore its topic fully, using whatever details, evidence, and examples are necessary. Without such development, a paragraph may seem lifeless and abstract.

Most good academic writing backs up general ideas with specifics. Shifting between the general and the specific is especially important at the paragraph level. If a paragraph contains nothing but specific details, its meaning may not be clear—but if a paragraph makes only general statements, it may seem boring or unconvincing.

Coherence

A paragraph has coherence—or flows—if its details fit together in a way that readers can easily follow. The following methods can help you achieve paragraph coherence:

- A general-to-specific or specific-to-general *organization* helps readers move from one point to another.

- *Repetition* of key words or phrases links sentences and suggests that the words or phrases are important.

- *Parallel structures* help make writing more coherent.

- *Transitions* such as *for example* and *however* help readers follow the progression of one idea to the next.

The same methods you use to create coherent paragraphs can be used to link paragraphs so that a whole piece of writing flows smoothly. You can create links to previous paragraphs by repeating or paraphrasing key words and phrases and by using parallelism and transitions.

Designing Texts

Because design elements help you get and keep the reader's attention and contribute to the tone of your text, they bring an important dimension to writing—what some call *visual rhetoric.*

Design Principles

Designer Robin Williams, in her *Non-Designer's Design Book*, identifies four principles that are a good starting point for making any print or digital text more effective.

Contrast: Begin with a focal point—a dominant visual or text that readers should look at first—and structure the flow of other information from that point. Use color, boldface or large type, white space, and so on to set off the focal point.

Alignment: Horizontal or vertical alignment of words and visuals gives a text a cleaner, more organized look. In general, wherever you begin aligning elements, stick with it throughout the text.

Repetition: Readers are guided in large part by the repetition of key words or design elements. Use color, type, style, and other visual elements consistently throughout a document.

Proximity: Parts of a text that are related should be physically close together (*proximate* to each other).

Appropriate Formats

Think about the most appropriate way to format a document to make it inviting and readable for your intended audience.

White space: Empty space, called "white space," guides the reader's eyes to parts of a page or screen. Provide ample margins and space between paragraphs; you can also use white space around particular content, such as a graphic or list, to make it stand out.

Color: Choose colors that relate to the purpose(s) of your text and its intended audience. For academic work, keep the number of colors fairly small to avoid a jumbled or confused look.

Paper: For print documents, choose paper that is an appropriate size and color for your purpose. For academic papers, put your last name and the page number in the upper-righthand corner of each page unless your instructor requires a different formatting style.

Type: Choose an easy-to-read type size and typeface, and be consistent in the styles and sizes of type used throughout your project. For most college writing, 11- or 12-point type is standard.

Spacing: Final drafts of printed academic writing should be double-spaced, with the first line of paragraphs indented one-half inch. Other documents, such as memos, letters, and Web texts, are usually single-spaced, with a blank line between paragraphs and no paragraph indentation. Some kinds of documents, such as newsletters, may call for multiple columns of text.

Headings: Consider organizing your text with headings that will aid comprehension. Some kinds of reports have standard headings (such as *Abstract*) that readers expect.

- Distinguish levels of headings using indents along with type. For example, you might center main headings and align lower-level headings at the left margin.

- Look for the most informative way to word your headings. You can state the topic in a single word (*Toxicity*); in a noun phrase (*Levels of Toxicity*) or gerund phrase (*Measuring Toxicity*); in a question to be answered in the text (*How Can Toxicity Be Measured?*); or in an imperative that tells readers what to do (*Measure the Toxicity*). Use the structure consistently for all headings of the same level.

Visuals

Choose visuals that will help make a point more vividly and succinctly than words alone. In some cases, visuals may be your primary text. Consider carefully what you want visuals to do for your writing. What will your audience want or need you to show?

If you are using a visual created by someone else, be sure to give appropriate credit and to get permission before using any visual that will be viewed in a public space.

Position and identification of visuals: Position visuals alongside or after the text that refers to them. Number your visuals (number tables separately from other visuals), and give them informative titles. In some instances, you may need to provide captions to give readers additional data such as source information.

Figure 1. College Enrollment for Men and Women by Age, 2007 (in millions)

Table 1. Word Choice by Race: *Seesaw and Teeter-totter*, Chicago, 1986

Manipulation of visuals: Technical tools available today make it relatively easy to manipulate visuals. As you would with any source material, carefully assess any visuals you find for effectiveness, appropriateness, and validity. If you choose to manipulate an image (cropping it, for example), do so responsibly and not in a way that makes the image misleading.

Reviewing, Revising, and Editing

Ask classmates or your instructor to review and respond to your draft, answering questions like these:

- What do you see as the major point, claim, or thesis?

- How convincing is the evidence? What can I do to support my thesis more fully?

- What points are unclear? How can I clarify them?

- How easy is it to follow my organization? How can I improve?

- What can I do to make my draft more interesting?

Revising means using others' comments along with your own analysis of the draft to make sure it is as complete, clear, and effective as possible. These questions can help you revise:

- How does the draft accomplish its purpose?

- Is the thesis clearly stated, and does it contain a topic and a comment?

- How does the introduction catch readers' attention?

- Will the draft interest and appeal to its audience?

- How does the draft indicate your stance on the topic?

- What are the main points that illustrate or support the thesis? Are they clear? Do you need to add material to the points or add new points?

- Are the ideas presented in an order that will make sense to readers?

- Are the points clearly linked by logical transitions?

- Have you documented your research appropriately?

- How are visuals, media, and research sources (if any) integrated into your draft?

- How does the draft conclude? Is the conclusion memorable?

Once you are satisfied with your revised draft's big picture, edit your writing to make sure that every detail is as correct as you can make it.

- Read your draft aloud to make sure it flows smoothly and to find typos or other mistakes.

- Are your sentences varied in length and in pattern or type?

- Have you used active verbs and effective language?

- Are all sentences complete and correct?

- Have you used the spell checker—and double-checked its recommendations?

- Have you chosen an effective design and used white space, headings, and color appropriately?

- Have you proofread one last time, going word for word?

Reflecting

Thinking back on what you've learned helps make that learning stick. The following questions can help you think about your development as a writer:

- What lessons have you learned from the writing? How will they help you with future writing projects?

- What aspects of your writing give you the most confidence? What needs additional work, and what can you do to improve?

- What confused you during this writing? How did you resolve your questions?

- Identify a favorite passage of your writing. What pleases you about it? Can you apply what you learn from this analysis to other writing situations?

- How would you describe your development as a writer?

Questions to Ask About Your Own Reading and Writing

- If this is an assigned reading, what are my *instructor's goals* in asking me to complete it?

- How does this reading fit into my instructor's plans for the class and/or into my current assignment or project?

- What are *my* goals for reading?

  - To understand the content and/or structure of the piece?

  - To follow the writer's moves, how the writer connects ideas?

  - To analyze evidence and/or sources?

  - To respond to the author's main point or argument?

  - To use this piece as part of my own research/writing?

  - Something else?

- Did I read the abstract and/or skim through any headings and/or visuals first?

- Have I underlined the central purpose or argument of the piece?

- Did I put down my highlighter and pick up my pen? Annotating in the margins and underlining key bits is more effective than large blocks of highlighting.

- Can I trace—through annotations in the margin, underlining topic sentences, or reverse outlining—the main points that support the author's purpose or argument?

  - Did I mark important or compelling parts of the piece?

  - Did I note questions or concerns?

  - Did I find a few key words, phrases, or quotes that I might like to discuss?

- What is my reaction to the piece? For example,

  - In what ways does the piece appeal to my emotions or values?

  - How does the use of evidence and reasoning in the piece affect my opinion of it?

  - What questions would I like to ask the author(s)?

- Have I considered the broader information and contexts for this piece?

  - Who is/are the author(s)? What purposes, motivations, and/or biases might the author(s) have?

  - Where was the piece published? What are the goals of that publication?

o   When was the piece published? How does its time context affect the argument, evidence, etc. in the piece?

o   What disciplinary perspective is the piece written from (social sciences, humanities, natural sciences, applied sciences)?

Developing and Structuring an Academic Argument

Before words ever reach a page, the writing process requires us to consider why we will be writing, what we will be writing, and the audience(s) for our writing. All of this consideration is known as "prewriting." The readings in this section address this step in the writing process. In "Invention" by Kirszner and Mandell, you are asked to set limits on your writing—this will help narrow your writing possibilities. You'll also read about specific tools to begin writing—such as the process for effective thesis development. "Arrangement," also by Kirszner and Mandell, walks readers through writing effective introductions, body paragraphs, and conclusions. Finally, "Arguments," by Ruszkiewicz and Dolmage, asks readers to explore the intricacies of prewriting and writing an argumentative essay. If the writing process has ever seemed daunting, or if you have ever asked yourself, "how and where do I start," this section should help guide your first steps.

Chapter Five

Invention

by Laurie G. Kirszner and Stephen R. Mandell

Invention, or **prewriting**, is an important (and, frequently, the most neglected) part of the writing process. At this stage, you discover what interests you about your subject and consider what ideas to develop in your essay.

When you are given a writing assignment, you may be tempted to start writing a first draft immediately. Before writing, however, you should be sure you understand your assignment and its limits, and you should think about what you want to say. Time spent on these issues now will pay off later when you draft your essay.

Understanding Your Assignment

Almost everything you write in college begins as an *assignment*. Some assignments will be direct and easy to understand:

> Write about an experience that changed your life.

> Discuss the procedure you used to synthesize ammonia.

Others will be difficult and complex:

> Using Jonathan Kozol's essay "The Human Cost of an Illiterate Society" as source material, write an essay using as your thesis the following statement by James Madison: "A people who mean to be their own governors must arm themselves with the power knowledge gives."

Before beginning to write, you need to understand what your assignment is asking you to do. If the assignment is written as a question, read it carefully several times, and underline its key words. If the assignment is read aloud by your instructor, be sure to copy it accurately. (A mistaken word—*analyze* for *compare*, for example—can make quite a difference.) If you are confused about anything, ask your instructor for clarification. Remember that no matter how well written an essay is, it will fall short if it does not address the assignment.

Setting Limits

Once you understand the assignment, you should consider its *length, purpose, audience*, and *occasion* and your own *knowledge* of the subject. Each of these factors helps you determine what you will say about your subject.

Length

Often, your instructor will specify the **length** of a paper, and this word or page limit has a direct bearing on your paper's focus. For example, you would need a narrower topic for a two-page essay than for a ten-page one. Similarly, you could not discuss a question as thoroughly during an hourlong exam as you might in a paper written over several days.

If your instructor sets no page limit, consider how the nature of the assignment suggests a paper's length. A *summary* of a chapter or an article, for instance, should be much shorter than the original, whereas an *analysis* of a poem will most likely be longer than the poem itself. If you are uncertain about the appropriate length for your paper, consult your instructor.

Purpose

Your **purpose** also limits what you say and how you say it. For example, if you were writing a job application letter, you would not emphasize the same elements of college life as you would in an email to a friend. In the first case, you would want to persuade the reader to hire you, so you might include your grade-point average, a list of the relevant courses you took, and perhaps the work you did for a service-learning course. In the second case, you would want to inform and perhaps entertain, so you might share anecdotes about dorm life or describe one of your favorite instructors. In each case, your purpose would help you determine what information to include to evoke a particular response in a specific audience.

In general, you can classify your purposes for writing according to your relationship to the audience.

- In **expressive writing**, you convey personal feelings or impressions to readers. Expressive writing is used in diaries, personal emails and journals, and often in narrative and descriptive essays as well.

- In **informative writing**, you inform readers about something. Informative writing is used in essay exams, lab reports, and expository essays as well as in some research papers and personal web pages.

- In **persuasive writing**, you try to convince readers to act or think in a certain way. Persuasive writing is used in editorials, argumentative essays, proposals, research papers, and many types of electronic documents such as blogs and web pages.

In addition to these general purposes, you might have a more specific purpose—to analyze, entertain, hypothesize, assess, summarize, question, report, recommend, suggest, evaluate, describe, recount, request, instruct, and so on. For example, suppose you wrote a report on homelessness in your community. Your general purpose might be to *inform* readers of the situation, but you might also want to *assess* the problem and *instruct* readers how to help those in need.

Audience

To be effective, your essay should be written with a particular **audience** in mind. An audience can be an *individual* (your instructor, for example), or it can be a *group* (like your classmates or coworkers). Your essay can address a *specialized* audience (such as a group of medical doctors or economists) or a *general* or *universal* audience whose members have little in common (such as the readers of a newspaper or magazine).

In college, your audience is usually your instructor, and your purpose in most cases is to demonstrate your mastery of the subject matter, your reasoning ability, and your competence as a writer. Other audiences may include classmates, professional colleagues, or members of your community. Considering the age and gender of your audience, its political and religious values, its social and educational level, and its interest in your subject may help you define it.

Often, you will find that your audience is just too diverse to be categorized. In such cases, many writers imagine a general (or universal) audience and make points that they think will appeal to a variety of readers. At other times, writers identify a common denominator, a role that characterizes the entire audience. For instance, when a report on the dangers of smoking asserts, "Now is the time for health-conscious individuals to demand that cigarettes be removed from the market," it automatically casts its audience in the role of health-conscious individuals.

After you define your audience, you have to determine how much (or how little) its members know about your subject. This consideration helps you decide how much information your readers will need in order to understand the discussion. Are they highly informed? If so, you can present your points without much explanation. Are they relatively uninformed? If this is the case, you will have to include definitions of key terms, background information, and summaries of basic research.

Keep in mind that experts in one field will need background information in other fields. If, for example, you were writing an analysis of Joseph Conrad's *Heart of Darkness*, you could assume that the literature instructor who assigned the novel would not need a plot summary. However, if you wrote an essay for your history instructor that used *Heart of Darkness* to illustrate the evils of European colonialism in nineteenth-century Africa, you would probably include a short plot summary. (Even though your history instructor would know a lot about colonialism in Africa, she might not be familiar with Conrad's work.)

Occasion

In general, **occasion** refers to the situation (or situations) that leads someone to write about a topic. Obviously, in an academic writing situation, the occasion is almost always a specific assignment. The occasion suggests a specific audience—for example, a history instructor—as well as a specific purpose—for example, to discuss the causes of World War I. In fact, even the format of a paper—whether you use (or do not use) headings or whether you present your response to an assignment as an essay, as a technical report, or as a PowerPoint presentation—is determined by the occasion for your writing. For this reason, a paper suitable for a psychology or sociology class might not be suitable for a composition class.

Like college writing assignments, each writing task you do outside of school requires an approach that suits the occasion. An email to coworkers, for instance, may be less formal than a report to a manager. In addition, the occasion suggests how much (or how little) information the piece of writing includes. Finally, your occasion suggests your purpose.

For example, an email to members of an online discussion group might be strictly informational, whereas an email to a state senator about preserving a local landmark would be persuasive as well as informative.

Knowledge

What you know (and do not know) about a subject determines what you can say about it. Before writing about any subject, ask yourself what you know about the subject and what you need to find out.

Different writing situations require different kinds of knowledge. A personal essay will draw on your own experiences and observations; a term paper will require you to gain new knowledge through research. In many cases, your page limit and the amount of time you are given to do the assignment will help you decide how much information you need to gather before you can begin.

Checklist: Setting Limits

Length

❏ Has your instructor specified a length?

❏ Does the nature of your assignment suggest a length?

Purpose

❏ Is your general purpose to express personal feelings? To inform? To persuade?

❏ In addition to your general purpose, do you have any more specific purposes?

❏ Does your assignment provide any guidelines about purpose?

Audience

❏ Is your audience a group or an individual?

❏ Are you going to address a specialized or a general audience?

❏ Should you take into consideration the audience's age, gender, education, biases, or political or social values?

❏ Should you cast your audience in a particular role?

❏ How much can you assume your audience knows about your subject?

Occasion

❏ Are you writing in class or at home?

❏ Are you addressing a situation outside the academic setting?

❏ What special approaches does your occasion for writing require?

Knowledge

❏ What do you know about your subject?

❏ What do you need to find out?

Moving from Subject to Topic

Although many essays begin as specific assignments, some begin as broad areas of interest or concern. These **general subjects** always need to be narrowed to **specific topics** that can be discussed within the limits of the assignment. For example, a subject like stem-cell research could be interesting, but it is too complicated to write about for any college assignment except in a general way. You need to limit such a subject to a topic that can be covered within the time and space available.

General Subject	Specific Topic
Stem-cell research	Using stem-cell research to cure multiple sclerosis
Herman Melville's *Billy Budd*	Billy Budd as a Christ figure
Constitutional law	One unforeseen result of the *Miranda* ruling
The Internet	The uses of chat rooms in composition classes

Two strategies can help you narrow a general subject to a specific topic: *questions for probing* and *freewriting*.

Questions for Probing

One way to move from a general subject to a specific topic is to examine your subject by asking a series of questions about it. These **questions for probing** are useful because they reflect how your mind operates—for instance, finding similarities and differences, or dividing a whole into its parts. By asking the questions on the following checklist, you can explore your subject systematically. Not all questions will work for every subject, but any single question may elicit many different answers, and each answer is a possible topic for your essay.

Checklist: Questions for Probing

- ❏ What happened?
- ❏ When did it happen?
- ❏ Where did it happen?
- ❏ Who did it?
- ❏ What does it look like?
- ❏ What are its characteristics?
- ❏ What impressions does it make?
- ❏ What are some typical cases or examples of it?
- ❏ How did it happen?
- ❏ What makes it work?
- ❏ How is it made?
- ❏ Why did it happen?
- ❏ What caused it?
- ❏ What does it cause?
- ❏ What are its effects?
- ❏ How is it like other things?
- ❏ How is it different from other things?
- ❏ What are its parts or types?
- ❏ How can its parts or types be separated or grouped?
- ❏ Do its parts or types fit into a logical order?
- ❏ Into what categories can its parts or types be arranged?
- ❏ On what basis can it be categorized?
- ❏ How can it be defined?
- ❏ How does it resemble other members of its class?
- ❏ How does it differ from other members of its class?

When applied to a subject, some of these questions can yield many workable topics, including some you might never have considered had you not asked the questions. For example, by applying this approach to the general subject "the Brooklyn Bridge," you can generate more ideas and topics than you need:

What happened? A short history of the Brooklyn Bridge

What does it look like? A description of the Brooklyn Bridge

How is it made? The construction of the Brooklyn Bridge

What are its effects? The impact of the Brooklyn Bridge on American writers

How does it differ from other members of its class? Innovations in the design of the Brooklyn Bridge

At this point in the writing process, you want to come up with possible topics, and the more ideas you have, the wider your choice. Begin by jotting down all the topics you think of. (You can repeat the process of probing several times to limit topics further.) Once you have a list of topics, eliminate those that do not interest you or are too complex or too simple to fit your assignment. When you have discarded these less promising topics, you should still have several left. You can then select the topic that best suits your paper's length, purpose, audience, and occasion, as well as your interests and your knowledge of the subject.

Tech Tip: Questions for Probing

You can store the questions for probing in a file that you can open whenever you have a new subject. Make sure you keep a record of your answers. If the topic you have chosen is too difficult or too narrow, you can return to the questions-for-probing file and probe your subject again.

Freewriting

Another strategy for moving from subject to topic is **freewriting**. You can use freewriting at any stage of the writing process—for example, to generate supporting information or to find a thesis. However, freewriting is a particularly useful way to narrow a general subject or assignment.

When you freewrite, you write for a fixed period, perhaps five or ten minutes, without stopping and without paying attention to spelling, grammar, or punctuation. Your goal is to get your ideas down on paper so that you can react to them and shape them. If you have nothing to say, write down anything until ideas begin to emerge—and in time they will. The secret is to *keep writing*. Try to focus on your subject, but don't worry if you wander off in other directions. The object of freewriting is to let your ideas flow. Often, your best ideas will come from the unexpected connections you make as you write.

After completing your freewriting, read what you have written and look for ideas you can write about. Some writers underline ideas they think they might explore in their essays. Any of these ideas could become essay topics, or they could become subjects for other freewriting exercises. You might want to freewrite again, using a new idea as your focus. This process of writing more and more specific freewriting exercises—called **focused freewriting** or **looping**—can often yield a great deal of useful information and help you decide on a workable topic.

Tech Tip: Freewriting

If you freewrite on a computer, you may find that staring at your own words causes you to go blank. One possible solution is to turn down the brightness until the screen becomes dark and then to freewrite. This technique allows you to block out distracting elements and concentrate on just your ideas. Once you finish freewriting, turn up the brightness, and see what you have.

A Student Writer: Freewriting

After reading, highlighting, and annotating Henry Louis Gates Jr.'s "'What's in a Name?'", Laura Bobnak, a student in a composition class, decided to write an essay in response to this Writing Workshop question.

> Write about a time when you, like Gates's father, could have spoken out in protest but chose not to. Would you make the same decision today?

In an attempt to narrow this assignment to a workable topic, Laura did the following freewriting exercise.

```
Write for ten minutes … ten minutes … at 9 o'clock in the morn-
ing—Just what I want to do in the morning—If you can't think of
something to say, just write about anything. Right! Time to get
this over with—An experience—should have talked—I can think of
plenty of times I should have kept quiet! I should have brought
a bottle of water to class. I wonder what the people next to me
are writing about. That reminds me. Next to me. Jeff Servin in
chemistry. The time I saw him cheating. I was mad but I didn't
do anything. I studied so hard and all he did was cheat. I was
so mad. Nobody else seemed to care. What's the difference between
now and then? It's only a year and a half ….Honor code? Maturity?
A lot of people cheated in high school. I bet I could write about
this—Before and after, etc. My attitude then and now.
```

After some initial floundering, Laura discovered an idea that could be the basis for her essay. Although her discussion of the incident still had to be developed, Laura's freewriting helped her discover a possible topic for her essay: a time she saw someone cheating and did not speak out.

Finding Something to Say

Once you have narrowed your subject to a workable topic, you need to find something to say about it. *Brainstorming* and *journal writing* are useful tools for generating ideas, and both can be helpful at this stage of the writing process (and whenever you need to find additional material).

Brainstorming

Brainstorming is a way of discovering ideas about your topic. You can brainstorm in a group, exchanging ideas with several students in your composition class and noting the most useful ideas. You can also brainstorm on your own, quickly recording every fact, idea, or detail you can think of that relates to your topic. Your notes might include words, phrases, statements, questions, or even drawings or diagrams. Jot them down in the order in which you think of them. Some of the items may be inspired by your class notes; others may be ideas you got from reading or from talking with friends; and still other items may be ideas you have begun to wonder about, points you thought of while moving from subject to topic, or thoughts that occurred to you as you brainstormed.

A Student Writer: Brainstorming

To narrow her topic further and find something to say about it, Laura Bobnak made the brainstorming notes shown on page 101. After reading these notes several times, Laura decided to concentrate on the differences between her current and earlier attitudes toward cheating. She knew that she could write a lot about this idea and relate it to the assignment, and she felt confident that her topic would be interesting both to her instructor and to the other students in the class.

Tech Tip: Brainstorming

Your word-processing program makes it easy to create bulleted or numbered lists and gives you the flexibility to experiment with different ways of arranging and grouping items from your brainstorming notes. You can even use the drawing tools to make diagrams.

Journal Writing

Journal writing can be a useful source of ideas at any stage of the writing process. Many writers routinely keep a journal, jotting down experiences or exploring ideas they may want to use when they write. They write journal entries even when they have no particular writing project in mind. Often, these journal entries are the kernels from which longer pieces of writing develop. Your instructor may ask you to keep a writing journal, or you may decide to do so on your own. In either case, you will find your journal entries are likely to be more narrowly focused than freewriting or brainstorming, perhaps examining a small part of a reading selection or even one particular statement. Sometimes you will write in your journal in response to specific questions, such as the Journal Entry assignments that appear throughout this book. Assignments like these can help you start thinking about a reading selection that you may later discuss in class or write about.

A Student Writer: Journal Writing

In the following journal entry, Laura Bobnak explores one idea from her brainstorming notes—her thoughts about her college's honor code.

> At orientation, the dean of students talked about the college's honor code. She talked about how we were a community of scholars who were here for a common purpose—to take part in an intellectual conversation. According to her, the purpose of the honor code is to make sure this conversation continues uninterrupted. This idea sounded dumb at orientation, but now it makes sense. If I saw someone cheating, I'd tell the instructor. First, though, I'd ask the student to go to the instructor. I don't see this as "telling" or "squealing." We're all here to get an education, and we should be able to assume everyone is being honest and fair. Besides, why should I go to all the trouble of studying while someone else does nothing and gets the same grade?

Even though Laura eventually included only a small part of this entry in her paper, writing in her journal helped her focus her ideas about her topic.

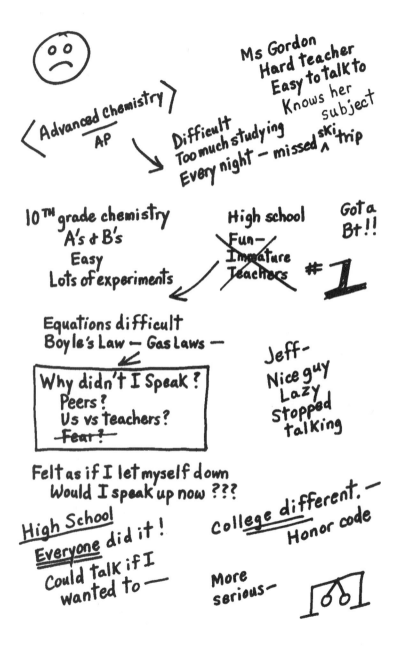

Figure 1. Brainstorming notes

Tech Tip: Keeping a Journal

Keeping your journal in a computer file has some obvious advantages. Not only can you maintain a neat record of your ideas, but you can also easily move entries from your journal into an essay without retyping them. Make sure, however, that you clearly distinguish between your ideas and those of your sources. If you paste material from your sources directly into your journal and then paste that material into your paper without documenting it, you are committing plagiarism.

Grouping Ideas

Once you have generated material for your essay, you will want to group ideas that belong together. *Clustering* and *outlining* can help you do this.

Clustering

Clustering is a way of visually arranging ideas so that you can tell at a glance where ideas belong and whether or not you need more information. Although you can use clustering at an earlier stage of the writing process, it is especially useful now for seeing how your ideas fit together. (Clustering can also help you narrow your paper's topic even further. If you find that your cluster diagram is too detailed, you can write about just one branch of the cluster.)

Begin clustering by writing your topic in the center of a sheet of paper. After circling the topic, surround it with the words and phrases that identify the major points you intend to discuss. (You can get ideas from your brainstorming notes, from your journal, and from your freewriting.) Circle these words and phrases, and connect them to the topic in the center. Next, construct other clusters of ideas relating to each major point, and draw lines connecting them to the appropriate point. By dividing and subdividing your points, you get more specific as you move outward from the center. In the process, you identify the facts, details, examples, and opinions that illustrate and expand your main points.

A Student Writer: Clustering

Because Laura Bobnak was not very visually oriented, she chose not to use this method of grouping her ideas. If she had, however, her cluster diagram might have looked like this.

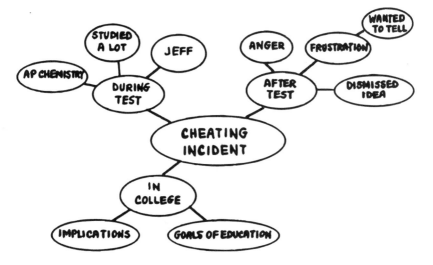

Making an Informal Outline

As an alternative or follow-up to clustering, you can organize your notes from brainstorming or other invention techniques into an **informal outline**. Informal outlines do not include all the major divisions and subdivisions of your paper the way formal outlines do; they simply suggest the shape of your emerging essay. Quite often an informal outline is just a list of your major points presented in a tentative order. Sometimes, however, an informal outline will include supporting details or suggest a pattern of development.

Tech Tip: Making an Informal Outline

You can easily arrange the notes you generated in your invention activities into an informal outline. You can construct an informal outline by typing words or phrases from your notes and rearranging them until the order makes sense. Later, you can use the categories from this informal outline to construct a formal outline.

A Student Writer: Making an Informal Outline

The following informal outline shows how Laura Bobnak grouped her ideas.

```
During test
    Found test hard
    Saw Jeff cheating
After test
    Got angry
    Wanted to tell
    Dismissed idea
In college
    Understand implications of cheating
    Understand goals of education
```

Understanding Thesis and Support

Once you have grouped your ideas, you need to consider your essay's thesis. A **thesis** is the main idea of your essay, its central point. The concept of *thesis and support*—stating your thesis and developing ideas that explain and expand it—is central to college writing.

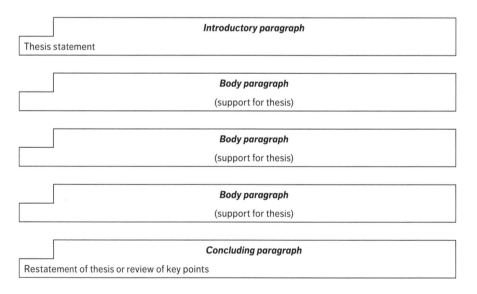

The essays you write will consist of several paragraphs: an **introduction** that presents your thesis statement, several **body paragraphs** that develop and support your thesis, and a **conclusion** that reinforces your thesis and provides closure. Your thesis holds this structure together; it is the center that the rest of your essay develops around.

Developing a Thesis

Defining the Thesis Statement

A **thesis statement** is more than a *title*, an *announcement of your intent*, or a *statement of fact*. Although a descriptive title orients your readers, it is not detailed enough to reveal your essay's purpose or direction. An announcement of your intent can reveal more, but it is stylistically distracting. Finally, a statement of fact—such as a historical fact or a statistic—is a dead end and therefore cannot be developed into an essay. For example, a statement like "Alaska became a state in 1959" or "Tuberculosis is highly contagious" or "The population of Greece is about ten million" provides your essay with no direction. However, a judgment or opinion *can* be an effective thesis—for instance, "The continuing threat of tuberculosis, particularly in the inner cities, suggests it is necessary to frequently test high-risk populations."

Title	Hybrid Cars: Pro and Con
Announcement of Intent	I will examine the pros and cons of hybrid cars that use both gasoline and electricity.
Statement of fact	Hybrid cars are more energy efficient than cars with standard gasoline engines.
Thesis statement	Hybrid cars that use both gasoline and electricity would decrease our country's dependence on foreign oil.
Title	Orwell's "A Hanging"
Announcement of Intent	This paper will discuss George Orwell's attitude toward the death penalty in his essay "A Hanging."
Statement of fact	In his essay, Orwell describes a hanging that he witnessed in Burma.
Thesis statement	In "A Hanging," George Orwell shows that capital punishment is not only brutal but also immoral.
Title	Speaking Out
Announcement of Intent	This essay will discuss a time when I could have spoken out but did not.
Statement of fact	Once I saw someone cheating and did not speak out.
Thesis statement	As I look back at the cheating I witnessed, I wonder why I kept silent and what would have happened if I had acted.

What a Good Thesis Does

For writers

It helps writers plan an essay.
It helps writers organize ideas in an essay.
It helps writers unify all the ideas in an essay.

For readers

It identifies the main idea of an essay.
It guides readers through an essay.
It clarifies the subject and the focus of an essay.

Deciding on a Thesis

No rules determine when you formulate your thesis; the decision depends on the scope of your assignment, your knowledge of the subject, and your method of writing. When you know a lot about a subject, you may come up with a thesis before doing any invention activities (freewriting or brainstorming, for example). At other times, you may have to review your notes and then think of a single statement that communicates your position on the topic. Occasionally, your assignment may specify a thesis by telling you to take a particular position on a topic. In any case, you should decide on a thesis statement before you begin to write your first draft.

As you write, you will continue to discover new ideas, and you will probably move in directions that you did not anticipate. For this reason, the thesis statement you develop at this stage of the writing process is only **tentative**. Still, because a tentative thesis helps you to focus your ideas, it is essential at the initial stages of writing. As you draft your essay, review your thesis statement in light of the points you make, and revise it accordingly.

Stating Your Thesis

It is a good idea to include a one-sentence statement of your thesis early in your essay. An effective thesis statement has three characteristics:

1. **An effective thesis statement clearly expresses your essay's main idea.** It does more than state your topic; it indicates what you will say about your topic, and it signals how you will approach your material. The following thesis statement, from the essay "Grant and Lee: A Study in Contrasts" by Bruce Catton, clearly communicates the writer's main idea.

    > They [Grant and Lee] were two strong men, these oddly different generals, and they represented the strengths of two conflicting currents that, through them, had come into final collision.

This statement says that the essay will compare and contrast Grant and Lee. Specifically, it indicates that Catton will present the two Civil War generals as symbols of two opposing historical currents. If the statement had been less fully developed—for example, had Catton written, "Grant and Lee were quite different from each other"—it would have just echoed the essay's title.

2. **An effective thesis statement communicates your essay's purpose.** Whether your purpose is to evaluate or analyze or simply to describe or inform, your thesis statement should communicate that purpose to your readers. In general terms, your thesis can be **expressive**, conveying a mood or impression; it can be **informative**, perhaps listing the major points you will discuss or presenting an objective overview of the essay; or it can be **persuasive**, taking a strong stand or outlining the position you will argue.

Each of the following thesis statements communicates a different purpose.

To express feelings	The city's homeless families live in heartbreaking surroundings.
To inform	The plight of the homeless has become so serious that it is a major priority for many city governments.
To persuade	The best way to address the problems of the homeless is to renovate abandoned city buildings to create suitable housing for homeless families.

3. **An effective thesis statement is clearly worded.** To communicate your essay's main idea, an effective thesis statement should be clearly worded. (It should also speak for itself. It is not necessary to write, "My thesis is that…" or "The thesis of this paper is…") The thesis statement should give a straightforward and accurate indication of what follows, and it should not mislead readers about the essay's direction, emphasis, scope, content, or viewpoint. Vague language, confusing abstractions, irrelevant details, and unnecessarily complex terminology have no place in a thesis statement. Keep in mind, too, that your thesis statement should not make promises that your essay is not going to keep. For example, if you are going to discuss just the *effects* of new immigration laws, your thesis statement should not emphasize the events that resulted in their passage.

Your thesis statement cannot, of course, include every point you will discuss in your essay. Still, it should be specific enough to indicate your direction and scope. The sentence "New immigration laws have failed to stem the tide of illegal immigrants" is not an effective thesis statement because it does not give your essay much focus.

Which immigration laws will you be examining? Which illegal immigrants? The following sentence, however, *is* an effective thesis statement. It clearly indicates what the writer is going to discuss, and it establishes a specific direction for the essay.

> Because they do not take into account the economic causes of immigration, current immigration laws do little to decrease the number of illegal immigrants coming from Mexico into the United States.

Implying a Thesis

Like an explicitly stated thesis, an **implied thesis** conveys an essay's purpose, but it does not do so explicitly. Instead, the selection and arrangement of the essay's ideas suggest the purpose. Professional writers sometimes prefer this option because an implied thesis is subtler than a stated thesis. (An implied thesis is especially useful in narratives, descriptions, and some arguments, where an explicit thesis would seem heavy-handed or arbitrary.) In most college writing, however, you should state your thesis to avoid any risk of being misunderstood or of wandering away from your topic.

Chapter Six

Arrangement

by Laurie G. Kirszner and Stephen R. Mandell

Each of the tasks discussed in Chapter 5 represents choices you have to make about your topic and your material. Now, before you actually begin to write, you have another choice to make—how to arrange your material into an essay.

Recognizing a Pattern

Sometimes arranging your ideas will be easy because your assignment specifies a particular pattern of development. This may be the case in a composition class, where the instructor may assign a descriptive or a narrative essay. Also, certain assignments or exam questions suggest how your material should be structured. For example, an instructor might ask you to tell about how something works, or an exam question might ask you to trace the circumstances leading up to an event. If you are perceptive, you will realize that your instructor is asking for a process essay and that the exam question is asking for either a narrative or a cause-and-effect response. The important thing is to recognize the clues such assignments give (or those you find in your topic or thesis statement) and to structure your essay accordingly.

One clue to structuring your essay can be found in the questions that proved most helpful when you probed your subject (see pages 95–97). For example, if questions like "What happened?" and "When did it happen?" yielded the most useful information about your topic, you should consider structuring your paper as a narrative. The chart on page 111 links various questions to the patterns of development they suggest. Notice that the terms in the right-hand column—narration, description, and so on—identify patterns of development that can help order your ideas.

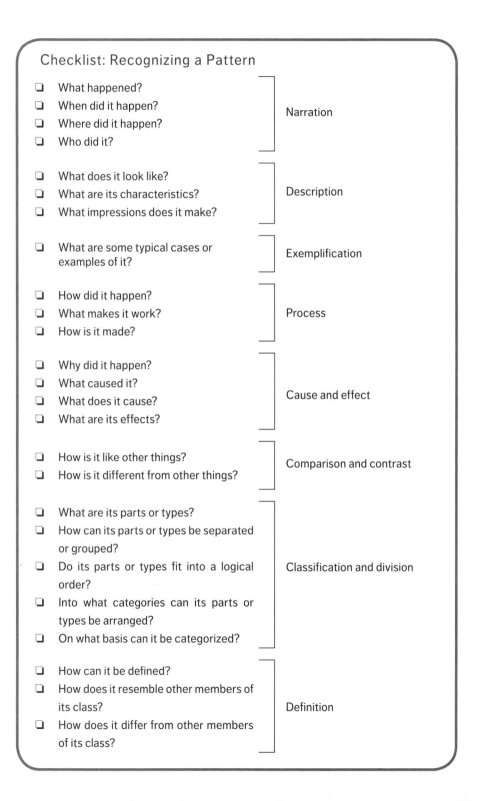

Checklist: Recognizing a Pattern

- ❏ What happened?
- ❏ When did it happen?
- ❏ Where did it happen?
- ❏ Who did it?

Narration

- ❏ What does it look like?
- ❏ What are its characteristics?
- ❏ What impressions does it make?

Description

- ❏ What are some typical cases or examples of it?

Exemplification

- ❏ How did it happen?
- ❏ What makes it work?
- ❏ How is it made?

Process

- ❏ Why did it happen?
- ❏ What caused it?
- ❏ What does it cause?
- ❏ What are its effects?

Cause and effect

- ❏ How is it like other things?
- ❏ How is it different from other things?

Comparison and contrast

- ❏ What are its parts or types?
- ❏ How can its parts or types be separated or grouped?
- ❏ Do its parts or types fit into a logical order?
- ❏ Into what categories can its parts or types be arranged?
- ❏ On what basis can it be categorized?

Classification and division

- ❏ How can it be defined?
- ❏ How does it resemble other members of its class?
- ❏ How does it differ from other members of its class?

Definition

Understanding the Parts of the Essay

No matter what pattern of development you use, your essay should have a beginning, a middle, and an end—that is, an *introduction*, a *body*, and a *conclusion*.

The Introduction

The **introduction** of your essay, usually one paragraph and rarely more than two, introduces your subject, creates interest, and often states your thesis.

You can use a variety of strategies to introduce an essay and engage your readers' interest. Here are several options for beginning an essay (in each paragraph, the thesis statement is underlined).

1. You can begin with ***background information***. This approach works well when you know the audience is already interested in your topic and you can come directly to the point. This strategy is especially useful for exams, where there is no need (or time) for subtlety.

    With inflation low, many companies have understandably lowered prices, and the oil industry should be no exception. Consequently, homeowners have begun wondering whether the high price of home heating oil is justified given the economic climate. It makes sense, therefore, for us to start examining the pricing policies of the major American oil companies. (economics essay)

2. You can introduce an essay with your own original ***definition*** of a relevant term or concept. This technique is especially useful for research papers or exams, where the meaning of a specific term is crucial.

    Democracy is a form of government in which power is given to and exercised by the people. This may be true in theory, but some recent elections have raised concerns about the future of democracy. Extensive voting-machine irregularities and "ghost voting" have jeopardized people's faith in the democratic process. (political science exam)

3. You can begin your essay with an ***anecdote*** or ***story*** that leads readers to your thesis.

    Three years ago, I went with my grandparents to my first auction. They live in a small town outside of Lancaster, Pennsylvania, where it is common for people to auction off the contents of a home when someone moves or dies. As I walked through the crowd, I smelled the funnel cakes frying in the food trucks, heard the hypnotic chanting of the auctioneer, and sensed the excitement of the crowd. Two hours later, I walked off with an old trunk that I had bought for thirty dollars and a passion for auctions that I still have today. (composition essay)

4. You can begin with a *question*.

What was it like to live through the Holocaust? Elie Wiesel, in *One Generation After*, answers this question by presenting a series of accounts about ordinary people who found themselves imprisoned in Nazi death camps. As he does so, he challenges some of the assumptions we have about the Holocaust and those who survived. (sociology book report)

5. You can begin with a *quotation*. If it arouses interest, it can encourage your audience to read further.

"The rich are different," F. Scott Fitzgerald said more than seventy years ago. Apparently, they still are. As an examination of the tax code shows, the wealthy receive many more benefits than the middle class or the poor do. (accounting paper)

6. You can begin with a *surprising statement*. An unexpected statement catches readers' attention and makes them want to read more.

Believe it or not, most people who live in the suburbs are not white and rich. My family, for example, fits into neither of these categories. Ten years ago, my family and I came to the United States from Pakistan. My parents were poor then, and by some standards, they are still poor even though they both work two jobs. Still, they eventually saved enough to buy a small house in the suburbs of Chicago. Throughout the country, there are many suburban families like mine who are working hard to make ends meet so that their children can get a good education and go to college. (composition essay)

7. You can begin with a *contradiction*. You can open your essay with an idea that most people believe is true and then get readers' attention by showing that it is inaccurate or ill advised.

Many people think that after the Declaration of Independence was signed in 1776, the colonists defeated the British army in battle after battle. This commonly held belief is incorrect. The truth is that the colonial army lost most of its battles. The British were defeated not because the colonial army was stronger, but because George Washington refused to be lured into a costly winner-take-all battle and because the British government lost interest in pursuing an expensive war three thousand miles from home. (history take-home exam)

8. You can begin with a **fact** or **statistic**.

> According to a recent government study, recipients of Medicare will spend billions of dollars on drugs over the next ten years. This is a very large amount of money, and it illustrates why lawmakers must do more to help older Americans with the cost of medications. <u>Although the current legislation is an important first step, more must be done to help the elderly afford the drugs they need.</u> (public policy essay)

No matter which strategy you select, your introduction should be consistent in tone with the rest of your essay. If it is not, it can misrepresent your intentions and even damage your credibility. (For this reason, it is a good idea not to write your introduction until after you have finished your rough draft.) A technical report, for instance, should have an introduction that reflects the formality and objectivity the occasion requires. The introduction to an autobiographical essay, however, should have a more informal, subjective tone.

Checklist: What Not to Do in an Introduction

❏ **Don't apologize.** Never use phrases such as "in my opinion" or "I may not be an expert, but…" By doing so, you suggest that you don't really know your subject.

❏ **Don't begin with a dictionary definition.** Avoid beginning an essay with phrases like "According to Webster's Dictionary…." This type of introduction is overused and trite. If you want to use a definition, develop your own.

❏ **Don't announce what you intend to do.** Don't begin with phrases such as "In this paper I will…" or "The purpose of this essay is to…." Use your introduction to create interest in your topic, and let readers discover your intention when they get to your thesis statement.

❏ **Don't wander.** Your introduction should draw readers into your essay as soon as possible. Avoid irrelevant comments or annoying digressions that will distract readers and make them want to stop reading.

The Body Paragraphs

The middle section, or **body**, of your essay develops your thesis. The body paragraphs present the support that convinces your audience your thesis is reasonable. To do so, each body paragraph should be *unified, coherent,* and *well developed*. It should also follow a particular pattern of development and should clearly support your thesis.

- *Each body paragraph should be unified.* A paragraph is **unified** when each sentence relates directly to the main idea of the paragraph. Frequently, the main idea of a paragraph is stated in a **topic sentence**. Like a thesis statement, a topic sentence acts as a guidepost, making it easy for readers to follow the paragraph's discussion. Although the placement of a topic sentence depends on a writer's purpose and subject, beginning writers often make it the first sentence of a paragraph.

Sometimes the main idea of a paragraph is not stated but **implied** by the sentences in the paragraph. Professional writers often use this technique because they believe that in some situations—especially narratives and descriptions—a topic sentence can seem forced or awkward. As a beginning writer, however, you will find it helpful to use topic sentences to keep your paragraphs focused.

Whether or not you include a topic sentence, remember that each sentence in a paragraph should develop the paragraph's main idea. If the sentences in a paragraph do not support the main idea, the paragraph will lack unity.

In the following excerpt from a student essay, notice how the topic sentence (underlined) unifies the paragraph by summarizing its main idea:

> Another problem with fast food is that it contains additives. Fast-food companies know that to keep their customers happy, they have to give them food that tastes good, and this is where the trouble starts. For example, to give fries flavor, McDonald's used to fry their potatoes in beef fat. Shockingly, their fries actually had more saturated fat than their hamburgers did. When the public found out how unhealthy their fries were, the company switched to vegetable oil. What most people don't know, however, is that McDonald's adds a chemical derived from animals to the vegetable oil to give it the taste of beef tallow.

The topic sentence, placed at the beginning of the paragraph, enables readers to grasp the writer's point immediately. The examples that follow all relate to that point, making the paragraph unified.

- *Each body paragraph should be coherent.* A paragraph is **coherent** if its sentences are smoothly and logically connected to one another. Coherence can be strengthened in three ways. First, you can repeat **key words** to carry concepts from one sentence to another and to echo important terms. Second, you can use **pronouns** to refer to key nouns in previous sentences. Finally, you can use **transitions**, words or expressions that show chronological sequence, cause and effect, and so on (see the list of transitions on page 117). These three strategies for connecting sentences—which you can also use to connect paragraphs within an essay—indicate for your readers the exact relationships among your ideas.

The following paragraph, from George Orwell's "Shooting an Elephant", uses repeated key words, pronouns, and transitions to achieve coherence.

I got up. The Burmans were already racing past me across the mud. It was obvious that the elephant would never rise again, but he was not dead. He was breathing very rhythmically with long rattling gasps, his great mound of a side painfully rising and falling. His mouth was wide open—I could see far down into the caverns of pale pink throat. I waited a long time for him to die, but his breathing did not weaken. Finally, I fired my two remaining shots into the spot where I thought his heart must be. The thick blood welled out of him like red velvet, but still he did not die. His body did not even jerk when the shots hit him, the tortured breathing continued without a pause. He was dying, very slowly and in great agony, but in some world remote from me where not even a bullet could damage him further. I felt that I had got to put an end to that dreadful noise. It seemed dreadful to see the great beast lying there, powerless to move and yet powerless to die, and not even to be able to finish him. I sent back for my small rifle and poured shot after shot into his heart and down his throat. They seemed to make no impression. The tortured gasps continued as steadily as the ticking of a clock.

TRANSITIONS

Sequence or addition

again	first,...second,...third	next
also	furthermore	one...another
and	in addition	still
besides	last	too
finally	moreover	

Time

afterward	finally	simultaneously
as soon as	immediately	since
at first	in the meantime	soon
at the same time	later	subsequently
before	meanwhile	then
earlier	next	until
eventually	now	

Comparison

also	in the same way	similarly
in comparison	likewise	

Contrast

although	in contrast	on the one hand...
but	instead	on the other hand...
conversely	nevertheless	still
despite	nonetheless	whereas
even though	on the contrary	yet
however		

Examples

for example	namely	that is
for instance	specifically	thus
in fact		

Conclusions or summaries

as a result	in summary
in conclusion	therefore
in short	thus

Causes or effects

as a result	so
because	then
consequently	therefore
since	

Orwell keeps his narrative coherent by using transitional expressions (*already, finally, when the shots hit him*) to signal the passing of time. He uses pronouns (*he, his*) in nearly every sentence to refer back to the elephant, the topic of his paragraph. Finally, he repeats key words like *shots* and *die* (and its variants *dead* and *dying*) to link the whole paragraph's sentences together.

- *Each body paragraph should be well developed.* A paragraph is **well developed** if it contains the **support**—examples, reasons, and so on—readers need to understand its main idea. If a paragraph is not adequately developed, readers will feel they have been given only a partial picture of the subject.

If you decide you need more information in a paragraph, you can look back at your brainstorming notes. If this doesn't help, you can freewrite or brainstorm again, talk with friends and instructors, read more about your topic, or (with your instructor's permission) do some research. Your assignment and your topic will determine the kind and amount of information you need.

Types of Support

- **Examples:** Specific illustrations of a general idea or concept
- **Reasons:** Underlying causes or explanations
- **Facts:** Pieces of information that can be verified or proved
- **Statistics:** Numerical data (for example, results of studies by reputable authorities or organizations)
- **Details:** Parts or portions of a whole (for example, steps in a process)
- **Expert opinions:** Statements by recognized authorities in a particular field
- **Personal experiences:** Events that you lived through
- **Visuals:** Diagrams, charts, graphs, or photographs

Checklist: Effective Support

❑ **Support should be relevant.** Body paragraphs should clearly relate to your essay's thesis. Irrelevant material—material that does not pertain to the thesis—should be deleted.

❑ **Support should be specific.** Body paragraphs should contain support that is specific, not general or vague. Specific examples, clear reasons, and precise explanations engage readers and communicate your ideas to them.

❑ **Support should be adequate.** Body paragraphs should contain enough facts, reasons, and examples to support your thesis. How much support you need depends on your audience, your purpose, and the scope of your thesis.

❑ **Support should be representative.** Body paragraphs should present support that is typical, not atypical. For example, suppose you write a paper claiming that flu shots do not work. Your support for this claim is that your grandmother got the flu even though she was vaccinated. This example is not representative because studies show that most people who get vaccinated do not get the flu.

❑ **Support should be documented.** Support that comes from research (print sources and the Internet, for example) should be documented. **Plagiarism**—failure to document the ideas and words of others—is not only unfair but also dishonest. Always use proper documentation to acknowledge your debt to your sources—and keep in mind that words and ideas you borrow from the essays in this book must also be documented.

The following student paragraph uses two examples to support its topic sentence.

Example 1

> Just look at how males have been taught that extravagance is a positive characteristic. Scrooge, the main character of Dickens's *A Christmas Carol*, is portrayed as an evil man until he gives up his miserly ways and freely distributes gifts and money on Christmas day. This behavior, of course, is rewarded when people change their opinions about him and decide that he isn't such a bad person after all.

Example 2

> Diamond Jim Brady is another interesting example. This individual was a nineteenth-century financier who was known for his extravagant taste in women and food. On any given night, he would eat enough food to feed at least ten of the numerous poor who roamed the streets of New York at that time. Yet, despite his selfishness and infantile self-gratification, Diamond Jim Brady's name has become associated with the good life.

- *Each body paragraph should follow a particular pattern of development.* In addition to making sure your body paragraphs are unified, coherent, and well developed, you need to organize each paragraph according to a specific pattern of development.

- *Each body paragraph should clearly support the thesis statement.* No matter how many body paragraphs your essay has—three, four, five, or even more—each paragraph should introduce and develop an idea that supports the essay's thesis. Each paragraph's topic sentence should express one of these supporting points. The diagram on page 121 illustrates this thesis-and-support structure.

Introductory paragraph

> *Thesis statement*: Despite the emphasis by journalists on objective reporting, there are <u>three reasons</u> why television news is anything but objective.

Body paragraph

> *Topic sentence:* Television news is not objective because the people who gather and report the news are biased.

Body paragraph

> *Topic sentence:* In addition, television news is not objective because networks face pressure from sponsors.

Body paragraph

> *Topic sentence:* Finally, television news is not objective because networks focus on ratings rather than content.

Concluding paragraph

> *Restatement of thesis:* Even though television journalists claim to strive for objectivity, the truth is that this ideal has been impossible to achieve.

The Conclusion

Since readers remember best what they read last, your **conclusion** is very important. Always end your essay in a way that reinforces your thesis and your purpose.

Like your introduction, your conclusion is rarely longer than a paragraph. Regardless of its length, however, your conclusion should be consistent with the rest of your essay— that is, it should not introduce points you have not discussed earlier. Frequently, a conclusion will restate your essay's main idea or review your key points.

Here are several strategies you can use to conclude an essay:

1. You can conclude your essay by ***reviewing your key points*** or ***restating your thesis***.

    Rotation of crops provided several benefits. It enriched soil by giving it a rest; it enabled farmers to vary their production; and it ended the cycle of "boom or bust" that had characterized the prewar South's economy when cotton was the primary crop. Of course, this innovation did not solve all the economic problems of the postwar South, but it did lay the groundwork for the healthy economy this region enjoys today. (history exam)

2.   You can end a discussion of a problem with a ***recommendation of a course of action***.

Well-qualified teachers are becoming harder and harder to find. For this reason, school boards should reassess their ideas about what qualifies someone to teach. At the present time, people who have spent their lives working in a particular field are denied certification because they have not taken education courses. This policy deprives school systems of talented teachers. In order to ensure that students have the best possible teachers, school boards should consider applicants' real-world experience when evaluating their qualifications. (education essay)

3.   You can conclude with a ***prediction***. Be sure, however, that your prediction follows logically from the points you have made in the essay. Your conclusion is no place to make new points or to change direction.

Campaign advertisements should help people understand a political candidate's qualifications and where he or she stands on critical issues. They should not appeal to people's fears or greed. Above all, they should not personally attack other candidates or oversimplify complex issues. If campaign advertisements continue to do these things, the American people will disregard them and reject the candidates they promote. (political science essay)

4.   You can end with a relevant ***quotation***.

In *Walden*, Henry David Thoreau says, "The mass of men lead lives of quiet desperation." This sentiment is reinforced by a drive through the Hill District of our city. Perhaps the work of the men and women who run the clinic on Jefferson Street cannot totally change this situation, but it can give us hope to know that some people, at least, are working for the betterment of us all. (public health essay)

Checklist: What Not to Do in a Conclusion

❏ **Don't end by repeating the exact words of your thesis and listing your main points.** Avoid boring endings that tell readers what they already know.

❏ **Don't end with an empty phrase.** Avoid ending with a cliché like "This just goes to prove that you can never be too careful."

❏ **Don't introduce new points or go off in new directions.** Your conclusion should not introduce new points for discussion. It should reinforce the points you have already made in your essay.

❏ **Don't end with an unnecessary announcement.** Don't end by saying that you are ending—for example, "In conclusion, let me say…" The tone of your conclusion should signal that the essay is drawing to a close.

Constructing a Formal Outline

Before you begin to write, you may decide to construct a **formal outline** to guide you. Whereas informal outlines are preliminary lists that simply remind you which points to make, formal outlines are detailed, multilevel constructions that indicate the exact order in which you will present your key points and supporting details. The complexity of your assignment determines which type of outline you need. For a short paper, an informal outline like the one on page 104 is usually sufficient. For a longer, more complex essay, however, you may need a formal outline.

One way to construct a formal outline is to copy down the main headings from your informal outline. Then, arrange ideas from your brainstorming notes or cluster diagram as subheadings under the appropriate headings. As you work on your outline, make sure each idea you include supports your thesis. Ideas that don't fit should be reworded or discarded. As you revise your essay, continue to refer to your outline to make sure your thesis and support are logically related. The guidelines that follow will help you prepare a formal outline.

Checklist: Constructing a Formal Outline

- ❏ Write your thesis statement at the top of the page.
- ❏ Group main headings under roman numerals (*I, II, III, IV*, and so on), and place them flush with the left-hand margin.
- ❏ Indent each subheading under the first word of the heading above it. Use capital letters before major points and numbers before supporting details.
- ❏ Capitalize the first letter of the first word of each heading.
- ❏ Make your outline as simple as possible, avoiding overly complex divisions of ideas. (Try not to go beyond third-level headings—*1, 2, 3*, and so on.)
- ❏ Construct either a **topic outline**, with headings expressed as short phrases or single words ("Advantages and disadvantages") or a **sentence outline**, with headings expressed as complete sentences ("The advantages of advanced placement chemistry outweigh the disadvantages"). *Never use both phrases and complete sentences in the same outline.*
- ❏ Express all headings at the same level in parallel terms. (If roman numeral *I* is a noun, *II, III,* and *IV* should also be nouns.)
- ❏ Make sure each heading contains at least two subdivisions. You cannot have a *1* without a *2* or an *A* without a *B*.
- ❏ Make sure your headings do not overlap.

Chapter Seven

Arguments

by John J. Ruszkiewicz and Jay T. Dolmage

It doesn't take much to spark an argument these days—a casual remark, a political observation, a dumb joke that hurts someone's feelings. Loud voices and angry gestures may follow, leaving observers upset and frustrated. But arguments aren't polarizing or hostile by nature, not when people are more interested in generating light than heat offers them. Arguments should make us smarter and better able to deal with problems in the world. In fact, you probably make such constructive arguments all the time without raising blood pressures, at least not too much.

Argument to advance a thesis	In an op-ed for the local paper, you *argue for the thesis* that people who talk on cell phones while driving are a greater hazard than drunk drivers because they are more numerous and more callous.
Refutation argument	In a term paper, you use facts and logic to *refute the argument* that students with college degrees will probably earn more in their lifetimes than students with only high school diplomas.
Visual argument	Rather than write a letter to the editor about out-of-control salaries for NCAA football coaches, you create a *visual argument*—an editorial cartoon—suggesting that a local coach is paid more than the entire faculty.

Deciding to Write an Argument

Arguments come in many shapes to serve different purposes. In your projects, you'll aim to do the following.

Offer levelheaded and disputable claims.   You won't influence audiences by making points no one cares about. Something consequential should be at stake in an argument you offer for public consumption. Maybe you want to change reader's minds about an issue that everyone else thinks has been settled. Or maybe you want to shore up what people already believe. In either case, you need a well-defined point, either stated or implied, if you hope to influence the kind of readers worth impressing: thoughtful, levelheaded people.

What claim does this ad from the Utah Department of Public Safety actually make? Might anyone dispute it? Do you find the ad effective visually? Utah Department of Highway Safety.

Offer good reasons to support a claim.   Without evidence and supporting reasons, a claim is just an assertion—and little better than a shout or a slogan. Slogans do have their appeal in advertising and politics. But they don't become arguments until they are backed by solid reasoning and a paper trail of evidence. No one said writing arguments is easy. Allow time for finding the facts.

Understand opposing claims and points of view.   You won't make a strong case of your own until you can *honestly* paraphrase the logic of those who see matters differently. Many people find that tough to do because it forces them to consider alternative points of view. But you will seem more credible when you acknowledge these other *reasonable* opinions even as you refute them. When you face less than rational claims, rebut them calmly but firmly. Avoid the impulse to respond with an insult or a petty comment of your own.

Frame arguments powerfully—and not in words only.   Sensible opinions still have to dress for the occasion: You need the right words and images to move a case forward. Fortunately, strategies for making effective arguments also cue you in to appeals that are less legitimate. We've all been seduced by claims just because they are stylish, hip, or repeated so often that they begin to seem true. But if such persuasion doesn't seem fair or sensible, that's all the more reason to reach for a higher standard in your own appeals.

Exploring Purpose and Topic

In a college assignment, you could be asked to write arguments about general topics related to courses, but you probably won't be told what your claims should be. That's your responsibility, based on your knowledge, experiences, and leanings. So choose subjects you genuinely care about—not issues the media or someone else defines as controversial. You'll do a more credible job defending your questionable choice *not* to wear a helmet when motorcycling than explaining, one more time, why the environment should concern us all. And if environmental matters do roil you, stake your claim on a well-defined ecological problem—perhaps from within your community—that you might actually influence by the power of your rhetoric.

If you really are stumped, the Yahoo! Directory's list of "Issues and Causes"—with topics from *abortion* to *zoos*—offers problems enough to keep pundits from MSNBC and Fox News buzzing to the end of the century. To find it, search "Society and Culture" or "Issues and Causes" on the site's main Web directory. ("Society and Culture" itself offers a menu of intriguing topic areas.) Once you have an issue or even a specific claim, your real work begins.

Learn much more about your subject.   Your first task is to do basic library and online research to get a better handle on your topic—*especially* when you think you already have all the answers. Chances are, you don't.

State a preliminary claim, if only for yourself.   Some arguments fail because writers never focus their thinking. They wander around vague topics, throwing out ideas or making contradictory assertions and leaving it to readers to assemble the random parts. To avoid this blunder, begin with a claim—a *complete* sentence that states a position you hope to defend. Such a statement will keep you on track as you explore a topic. Even a simple sentence helps:

> The college rankings published annually by *U.S. News & World Report* do more harm than good.

> People who oppose gay marriage don't know what they are talking about.

Qualify your claim to make it reasonable.   As you learn more about a subject, revise your topic idea to reflect the complications you encounter. Your thesis will probably grow longer or take several sentences to explain, but the topic itself will actually narrow because of the specific issues you've identified. You'll also have less work to do, thanks to qualifying expressions such as *some, most, a few, often, under certain conditions, occasionally, when necessary,* and so on. Other qualifying expressions are highlighted below.

> The **statistically unreliable** college ratings published by *U.S. News & World Report* **usually** do more harm than good to students **because** some claim that they lead admissions officers to award scholarships on the basis of merit rather than need.

> **Many conservative critics** who oppose gay marriage **unwittingly** undermine their own core principles, **especially monogamy and honesty**.

Examine your core assumptions.   Claims may be supported by reasons and evidence, but they are based on assumptions. *Assumptions* are the principles and values upon which we base our beliefs and actions. Sometimes these assumptions are controversial and stand right out. At other times, they're so close to us, they seem invisible—they are part of the air we breathe. Expect to spend a paragraph defending any assumptions your readers might find questionable or controversial.

Claim

The statistically unreliable college ratings published by *U.S. News & World Report* usually do more harm than good to students because some claim that they lead admissions officers to award scholarships on the basis of merit rather than need.

Arguments take many different forms, but finger-pointing is rarely a good persuasive tool.

Assumption

Alleviating need in our society is more important than rewarding merit. [Probably controversial]

Claim

Westerners should be more willing to defend their cultural values and intellectual achievements if they hope to defend freedom against its enemies.

Assumption

Freedom needs to be defended at all costs. [Possibly controversial for some audiences]

Claim

Many conservative critics who oppose gay marriage unwittingly undermine their own core principles, especially monogamy and honesty.

Assumption

People should be consistent about their principles. [Probably not controversial]

Understanding Your Audience

Retailers know audiences. In fact, they go to great lengths to pinpoint the groups most likely to buy their fried chicken or hybrid cars. They then tailor their brand images and Web advertising to precisely those customers. You'll play to audiences the same way when you write arguments—if maybe a little less cynically.

Understand that you won't ever please everyone in a general audience, even if you write bland, colorless mush—because some readers will then regard you as craven and spineless. In fact, how readers imagine you, *as the person presenting an argument*, may determine their willingness to consider your claims at all.

Consider and control your ethos.   People who study persuasion describe the identity that writers create for themselves within an argument as their *ethos*—the voice and attitude they fashion to enhance their appeal. It is a powerful concept, worth remembering. Surely you notice when writers are coming across as, let's say, ingratiatingly confident or stupidly obnoxious. And don't you respond in kind, giving ear to the likable voice and dismissing the malicious one? A few audiences—like those for political blogs—may actually prefer a writer with a snarky ethos. But most readers respond better when writers seem reasonable, knowledgeable, and fair—neither insulting those who disagree with them nor making those who share their views embarrassed to have them on their side.

You can shape your ethos by adjusting the style, tone, and vocabulary of your argument: For instance, contractions can make you seem friendly (or too casual); an impressive vocabulary suggests that you are smart (or maybe just pompous); lots of name-dropping makes you seem hip (or perhaps pretentious). You may have to write several drafts to find a suitable ethos for a particular argument. And, yes, your ethos may change from paper to paper, audience to audience.

Consider self-imposed limits.   If you read newspapers and magazines that mostly confirm your own political views, you might be in for a wake-up call when you venture an opinion beyond your small circle of friends. Tread softly. There are good reasons why people don't talk politics at parties. When you do argue about social, political, or religious issues, be respectful of those who work from premises different from your own.

Consider the worlds of your readers. When arguing about topics such as education, politics, art, economics, ethics, or even athletics, you'll quickly realize that people bring their entire lives into the discussion of such issues. Their views are shaped, in part, by their gender, race, ethnicity, sexual orientation, income, age, and upbringing—and more, and in ever-varying combinations. Dealing with such considerations, you should be sensitive but not gutless.

Men and women, for instance, whether straight or gay, may not inhabit quite the same worlds. But, even so, you shouldn't argue, either, as if all men and all women think the same way—or should.

People's lives are similarly defined by their economic situations—and the assumptions that follow from privilege, poverty, or something in between. Think it would be cool to

have an outdoor pool on campus or a convenient new parking garage? You may find other students less willing than you to absorb the impact such proposals might have on their tuition. And if you intend to complain about fat cats, ridicule soccer moms, or poke fun at rednecks, is it because you can't imagine people different from you among your readers?

Gender attitudes develop early, along with some argument strategies.

Obviously, age matters too: You'd write differently for children than for their parents on almost any subject, changing your style, vocabulary, and allusions. But consider that people of different ages really have lived different lives. Each generation grows up with shared attitudes, values, heroes, and villains. As a writer, you have to factor such considerations into the arguments you write.

Finding and Developing Materials

You could write a book from the materials you'll collect researching some arguments. Since arguments often deal with current events and topics, start with a resource such as the Yahoo! Directory's "Issues and Causes" list mentioned earlier. Explore your subject, too, in *LexisNexis*, if your library gives you access to this huge database of newspaper articles.

As you gather materials, though, consider how much space you have to make your argument. Sometimes a claim has to fit within the confines of a letter to the editor, an op-ed column in a local paper, or a fifteen-minute PowerPoint talk. Aristotle, still one of the best theorists on persuasion, thought arguments *should* be brief, with speakers limiting examples to the *minimum* necessary to make a case—no extra points for piling on. So gather big, and then select only the best stuff for your argument.

List your reasons.   You'll come up with reasons to support your claim almost as soon as you choose a subject. Write those down. Then start reading and continue to list new reasons as they arise, not being too fussy at this point. Be careful to paraphrase these ideas so that you don't inadvertently plagiarize them later.

Then, when your reading and research are complete, review your notes and try to group the arguments that support your position. It's likely you'll detect patterns and relationships among these reasons, and an unwieldy initial list of potential arguments may be streamlined into just three or four—which could become the key reasons behind your claim. Study these points and look for logical connections or sequences. Readers will expect your ideas to converge on a claim or lead logically toward it.

Assemble your hard evidence.   Gather examples, illustrations, quotations, and numbers to support each main point. Record these items as you read in some reliable way, keeping track of all bibliographical information (author, title, publication info, URL) just as you would when preparing a term paper—even if you aren't required to document your argument. You want that data on hand in case your credibility is challenged later.

If you borrow facts from a Web site, do your best to trace the information to its actual source. For example, if a blogger quotes statistics from the U.S. Department of Agriculture, find that table or graph on the USDA Web site itself and make sure the numbers reported are accurate.

Cull the best quotations.   You've done your homework for an assignment, reading the best available sources. So prove it in your argument by quoting from them intelligently. Choose quotations that do one or more of the following:

- Put your issue in focus or context.

- Make a point with special power and economy.

- Support a claim or piece of evidence that readers might doubt.

- State an opposing point well.

Copy passages that appeal to you, but don't figure on using all of them. An argument that is a patchwork of quotations reads like a patchwork of quotations—which is to say, *boring*. Be sure to copy the quotations accurately and be certain you can document them.

Find counterarguments.   If you study a subject thoroughly, you'll come across plenty of honest disagreement. List all reasonable objections you can find to your claim, either to your basic argument or to any controversial evidence you expect to cite. When possible, cluster these objections to reduce them to a manageable few. Decide which you must refute in detail, which you might handle briefly, and which you can afford to dismiss.

Watch, for example, how in an editorial, the *New York Times* anticipates objections to its defense of a *Rolling Stone* magazine cover (August 2013) featuring accused Boston Marathon bomber Dzhokhar Tsarnaev. The *Times* concedes that merchants and consumers alike might resist the cover, but then it counterpunches:

> Stores have a right to refuse to sell products because, say, they are unhealthy, like cigarettes.… Consumers have every right to avoid buying a magazine that offends them, like *Guns & Ammo* or *Rolling Stone*.
>
> But singling out one magazine issue for shunning is over the top, especially since the photo has already appeared in a lot of prominent places, including the front page of this newspaper, without an outcry. As any seasoned reader should know, magazine covers are not endorsements.
>
> — The Editorial Board, "Judging Rolling Stone by Its Cover," *New York Times*, July 18, 2013

Consider emotional appeals.   Feelings play a powerful role in many arguments, a fact you cannot afford to ignore when a claim you make stirs people up. Questions to answer about possible emotional appeals include the following:

- What emotions might be effectively raised to support my point?
- How might I responsibly introduce such feelings: through words, images, color, sound?
- How might any feelings my subject arouses work contrary to my claims or reasons?

Creating a Structure

It's easy to sketch a standard structure for arguments: one that leads from claim to supporting reasons to evidence and even accommodates a counterargument or two.

Introduction leading to a claim or thesis statement
First reason and supporting evidence (stronger)
Second reason and supporting evidence (strong)
Third reason and supporting evidence (strongest)
Counterarguments
Conclusion

The problem is that you won't read many effective arguments, either in or out of school, that follow this template. The structure isn't defective, just too simple to describe the way arguments really move when ideas matter. You won't write a horrible paper if you use the traditional model because all the parts will be in place. Thesis? Check. Three supporting reasons? Check. Counterarguments? Check. But you will sound exactly like what you are: A writer going through the motions instead of engaging with ideas. Here's how to get your ideas to breathe in an argument—while still hitting all the marks.

Make a point or build toward one.   Arguments can unfurl just as reports do, with unmistakable claims followed by reams of supporting evidence. But they can also work like crime dramas, in which the evidence in a case builds toward a compelling conclusion—your thesis perhaps. This is your call. But don't just jump into a claim: Take a few sentences or paragraphs to set up the situation. Quote a nasty politician or tell an eye-popping story or two. Get readers invested in what's to come.

Spell out what's at stake.   When you write an argument, you initiate a controversy, so you'd better explain it clearly. Do you hope to fix a looming problem? Then describe your concern and make readers share it. Do you intend to correct a false notion or bad reporting? Then tell readers why setting the record straight matters. Appalled by the apathy of voters, the dangers of global warming, the infringements of free speech on campus? Explain why readers should care.

Address counterpoints when necessary, not in a separate section.   *Necessary* is when your readers start thinking to themselves, "Yeah, but what about...?" Such doubts will probably surface approximately where your own do—and, admit it, you have some misgivings about your argument. So take them on. Strategically, it rarely makes sense to consign all objections to a lengthy section near the end of a paper. That's asking for trouble. Do you really want to offer a case for the opposition just when your readers are finishing up? On the plus side, dealing with opposing arguments can be like caffeine for your prose, sharpening your attention and reflexes.

Save your best arguments for the end.   Of course, you want strong points throughout the paper. But you need a high note early on to get readers interested and then another choral moment as you finish to send them out the door humming. If you must summarize an argument, don't let a dull recap of your main points squander an important opportunity to influence readers. End with a rhetorical flourish that reminds readers how compelling your arguments are.

A pithy phrase, an ironic twist, and a question to contemplate can also lock down your case. Here's Maureen Dowd, bleakly—and memorably—concluding an argument defending the job journalists had done covering the Iraq War:

> Journalists die and we know who they are. We know they liked to cook and play Scrabble. But we don't know who killed them, and their killers will never be brought to justice. The enemy has no face, just a finger on a detonator.

— "Live from Baghdad: More Dying," *New York Times*, May 31, 2006

Choosing a Style and Design

Arguments vary widely in style. An unsigned editorial you write to represent the opinion of a student newspaper might sound formal and serious. Composing an op-ed under your own name, you'd probably ease up on the dramatic metaphors and allow yourself more personal pronouns. Arguing a point in an alternative magazine, you might even slip into the lingo of its vegan or survivalist subscribers. Routine adjustments like these really matter when you need to attract and hold readers.

You should also write with sensitivity since some people reading arguments may well be wavering, defensive, or eager to be offended. There's no reason to distract them with fighting words if you want to offer a serious argument. Here's how political commentator Ann Coulter described a politically active group of 9/11 widows who she believed were using their status to shield their anti–Iraq War opinions from criticism:

> These broads are millionaires, lionized on TV and in articles about them, reveling in their status as celebrities and stalked by grief-arazzis. I have never seen people enjoying their husbands' deaths so much.
>
> — *Godless: The Church of Liberalism* (2006)

Any point Coulter might make simply gets lost in the viciousness of the attack.

There are many powerful and aggressive ways to frame an argument without resorting to provocative language or fallacies of argument. Some of these strategies follow.

Invite readers with a strong opening.   Arguments—like advertisements—are usually discretionary reading. People can turn away the moment they grow irritated or bored. So you may need to open with a little surprise or drama. Try a blunt statement, an anecdote, or a striking example if it helps—maybe an image too. Or consider personalizing the lead-in, giving readers a stake in the claim you are about to make. The following is a remarkable opening paragraph from an argument by Malcolm Gladwell on the wisdom of banning dogs by breed. When you finish, ask yourself whether Gladwell has earned your attention. Would you read the rest of the piece?

> One afternoon last February, Guy Clairoux picked up his two-and-a-half-year-old son, Jayden, from day care and walked him back to their house in the west end of Ottawa, Ontario. They were almost home. Jayden was straggling behind, and, as his father's back was turned, a pit bull jumped over a backyard fence and lunged at Jayden. "The dog had his head in its mouth and started to do this shake," Clairoux's wife, JoAnn Hartley, said later. As she watched in horror, two more pit bulls jumped over the fence, joining in the assault. She and Clairoux came running,

and he punched the first of the dogs in the head, until it dropped Jayden, and then he threw the boy toward his mother. Hartley fell on her son, protecting him with her body. "JoAnn!" Clairoux cried out, as all three dogs descended on his wife. "Cover your neck, cover your neck." A neighbor, sitting by her window, screamed for help. Her partner and a friend, Mario Gauthier, ran outside. A neighborhood boy grabbed his hockey stick and threw it to Gauthier. He began hitting one of the dogs over the head, until the stick broke. "They wouldn't stop," Gauthier said. "As soon as you'd stop, they'd attack again. I've never seen a dog go so crazy. They were like Tasmanian devils." The police came. The dogs were pulled away, and the Clairouxes and one of the rescuers were taken to the hospital. Five days later, the Ontario legislature banned the ownership of pit bulls. "Just as we wouldn't let a great white shark in a swimming pool," the province's attorney general, Michael Bryant, had said, "maybe we shouldn't have these animals on the civilized streets."

— "Troublemakers," *New Yorker*, February 6, 2006

Write vibrant sentences.   You can write arguments full throttle, using a complete range of rhetorical devices, from deliberate repetition and parallelism to dialogue and quotation. Metaphors, similes, and analogies fit right in too. The trick is to create sentences rich enough to keep readers hooked, yet lean enough to advance an argument. In the following three paragraphs, follow the underlining to see how Thomas L. Friedman uses parallelism and one intriguing metaphor after another to argue in favor of immigration legislation after witnessing the diversity in a high school graduation class in Maryland.

There is a lot to be worried about in America today: <u>a war</u> in Iraq that is getting worse not better, <u>an administration</u> whose fiscal irresponsibility we will be paying for for a long time, <u>an education system</u> that is not producing enough young Americans skilled in math and science, and <u>inner cities</u> where way too many black males are failing. We must work harder and get smarter if we want to maintain our standard of living.

But if there is one reason to still be optimistic about America it is represented by the stunning diversity of the Montgomery Blair class of 2006. America is still <u>the world's greatest human magnet</u>. We are not the only country that embraces diversity, but there is something about our free society and free market that still attracts people like no other. Our greatest asset is our ability to still <u>cream off</u> not only the <u>first-round intellectual draft choices</u> from around the world but the low-skilled, high-aspiring ones as well, and that is the main reason that I am not yet ready to cede the twenty-first century to China. Our Chinese will still beat their Chinese.

<u>This influx of brainy and brawny immigrants is our oil well</u>—one that never runs dry. It is an endless source of <u>renewable human energy and creativity</u>. Congress ought to stop debating gay marriage and finally give us a framework to maintain a free flow of legal immigration.

— "A Well of Smiths and Xias," *New York Times*, June 7, 2006

Ask rhetorical questions.   The danger of rhetorical questions is that they can seem stagy and readers might not answer them the way you want. But the device can be very powerful in hammering a point home. Good questions also invite readers to think about an issue in exactly the terms that a writer prefers. Here's George Will using rhetorical questions to conclude a piece on global warming:

In fact, the earth is always experiencing either warming or cooling. But suppose the scientists and their journalistic conduits, who today say they were so spectacularly wrong so recently, are now correct. Suppose the earth is warming and suppose the warming is caused by human activity. Are we sure there will be proportionate benefits from whatever climate change can be purchased at the cost of slowing economic growth and spending trillions? Are we sure the consequences of climate change—remember, a thick sheet of ice once covered the Midwest—must be bad? Or has the science-journalism complex decided that debate about these questions, too, is "over"?

— "Let Cooler Heads Prevail," *Washington Post*, April 2, 2006

Questions to Ask About Your Own Academic Argument

- Do I understand the requirements of the Researched Argument?

    o   Do I understand how the genre of the Researched Argument defines the parameters of the Researched argument?

    o   Do I understand the many modes of writing I will be engaging with in the Researched Argument (i.e., summary, analysis, comparison, etc)?

    o   Do I understand the limitations of the Researched Argument (length, topic, etc.)?

    o   How might the Researched Argument, written for the purpose of 1010, differ from a Researched Argument written in an introductory psychology or history class?

- Have I considered the purpose, audience, and occasion for the Researched Argument?

    o   If the purpose of the Researched Argument is to persuade my reader, then how does this affect how I conduct my research and write my essay?

    o   Is my audience a person, group, or a specialized audience? How much context (background information) about my subject will I need to provide for my audience?

    o   Do I expect my audience to already have a view or position on this topic? How do I want to shape or change any pre-existing views? Am I realistic about what I can accomplish with this argument?

- How much knowledge do I already have on my subject?

    o   Do I need to begin by understanding the basics of my subject? Or can I begin looking at scholarly articles? Recall we are not reporting on a topic; rather, we are formulating an original argument.

    o   Am I open to having my own views shaped by my research?

    o   What have I done to avoid "cherry picking" or "confirmation bias"—gathering research with the only goal of proving myself "right"?

- Have I refined my subject into an argument?

    o   How can I make my argument more specific or focused?

    o   How can I make my argument more nuanced and/or original?

    o   What do I *want to add* to the conversation about this topic? Invention activities such as brainstorming, freewriting, and clustering can help me move from subject to topic and from topic to argument.

- Do I have a working thesis for my Researched Argument?
  - Does my thesis clearly express the one controlling idea of my argument?
  - Does my thesis clearly express the purpose for my writing?
  - Is my thesis clear to my reader(s) and easy to identify?
- Have I chosen the best pattern or structure of the Research Argument?
  - Does my Researched Argument have a clear introduction, body, and conclusion?
  - How did I capture the attention and interest of my reader? Does my introduction begin with background information, a definition, an anecdote, a question, a quotation, a surprising statement, or a fact?
  - Does my introduction include my thesis statement?
  - Do my body paragraphs reflect my intended argument/purpose that I stated in my thesis?
  - Does each body paragraph either contain evidence, analysis, or a bit of both?
  - Does my conclusion *restate* my thesis in a strong, memorable way? Does it summarize the crux of my argument and key points?
- Have I presented counterarguments or alternative perspectives on this topic? Have I addressed how these alternative perspectives can be accepted as part of my argument, partially accepted or amended, or rebutted?
- Is each of my body/discussion paragraphs well developed?
  - Does each body paragraph have a clear topic sentence that states the main idea of the paragraph?
  - Are my body paragraphs unified? In other words, does each paragraph reflect the intended purpose of the paragraph that I stated in my topic sentence?
  - Are each of my body paragraphs coherent? In other words, do their main ideas flow together and connect to one another logically? Did I use transition words or phrases to help provide coherence within and between my paragraphs.
- Have I used sources appropriate for the audience, purpose, and occasion of this assignment? Have I chosen my sources carefully (see Section 4 of this book for more)?
- Have I integrated my sources into my text succcessfully by introducing and framing them (see Section 4 for more)?
- Have I structured my works cited and in-text citations carefully (see Section 4)?
- Have I proofread carefully (see Section 5)?

Working with Sources

Because writing goes hand-in-hand with researching and finding sources to complement your project, working with source materials is important. This section is about "secondary sources," things written by other people that you want to use to make your own project stronger. The process of incorporating sources into your work includes multiple steps: finding things that work with your topic, genre, purpose, audience, and contexts; deciding when and how to use the sources in your work; and documenting your sources. The readings in this section support the steps in this process. Documentation styles, such as MLA and APA, change over time. Make sure to find out what style your instructor is using, then find online sources to get the most up-to-date information on that style.

Chapter
Eight

Summarizing Sources, Paraphrasing Sources, and Incorporating Sources
by John J. Ruszkiewicz and Jay T. Dolmage

Summarizing Sources

Once you determine which materials deserve closer attention and you have read these articles, books, and other texts critically—with an eye toward using their insights and data in your research project—you're ready to summarize the individual items, putting ideas you've found into your own words. These brief summaries or fuller paraphrases can become the springboard for composing your paper.

Prepare a summary for every item you examine in a project. This advice seems self-evident, but it is not. A quick look may tell you that an article or book has no bearing on your project. Even so, describe it very briefly on a note card or in an electronic file (with complete bibliographic data). Such a record reminds you that you have, in fact, seen and reviewed that item—which can be no small comfort when working on projects that stretch over several weeks or months. After you've examined dozens and dozens of sources, it's easy to forget what exactly you've read.

Use a summary to recap what a writer has said. When a source is clearly relevant to your project, look carefully for its main point and build your summary on it, making sure that this statement *does* reflect the actual content of the source, not your opinion of it. Be certain that the summary is *entirely* in your own words. Include the author and title of the work, too, so you can easily cite it later. The following is one summary of a *USA Today* editorial, with all the required citation information:

> In "Sanity 101," the editors of *USA Today* (January 19, 2006) criticize current college admission practices, which, they argue, make students and parents alike fear that getting into an appropriate school is harder than it really is.

Source: "Sanity 101." Editorial. *USA Today* 19 Jan. 2006: 10A. Print.

Be sure your summary is accurate and complete.   Even when a source makes several points, moves in contradictory directions, or offers a complex conclusion, your job is simply to describe what the material does. Don't embellish the material or blur the distinction between the source's words and yours. Include all bibliographical information (title, author, and date) from the source. The following summary of "Sanity 101" shows what can go wrong if you are not careful.

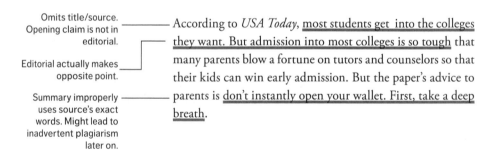

Omits title/source.
Opening claim is not in editorial.

Editorial actually makes opposite point.

Summary improperly uses source's exact words. Might lead to inadvertent plagiarism later on.

According to *USA Today*, <u>most students get into the colleges they want. But admission into most colleges is so tough</u> that many parents blow a fortune on tutors and counselors so that their kids can win early admission. But the paper's advice to parents is <u>don't instantly open your wallet. First, take a deep breath</u>.

Use a summary to record your take on a source.   In addition to reporting the contents of the material accurately, note also how the source might (or might not) contribute to your paper. But make certain that your comments won't be confused with claims made in the summarized article itself. The following are two acceptable sample summaries for "Sanity 101."

> In "Sanity 101," *USA Today* (January 19, 2006) describes the efforts of college applicants and parents to deal with the progressively more competitive admissions policies of elite institutions. The editorial claims that most schools, however, are far less selective. The article includes a reference to another *USA Today* piece by Mary Beth Marklein on the support some companies offer employees to assist them with college admissions issues.

Source: "Sanity 101." Editorial. *USA Today* 19 Jan. 2006: 10A. Print.

In an editorial (January 19, 2006) entitled "Sanity 101," *USA Today* counsels parents against worrying too much about hypercompetitive current college admission practices. In reality, only a small percentage of schools are highly selective about admissions. The editorial doesn't provide the schools' side of the issue.

Source: "Sanity 101." Editorial. *USA Today* 19 Jan. 2006: 10A. Print.

Use summaries to prepare an annotated bibliography.   In an annotated bibliography, brief summaries are provided for every item in an alphabetical list of sources. These summaries help readers understand the content and scope of materials.

Paraphrasing Sources

Paraphrases provide more complete records of the research materials you examine than do summaries. Like a summary, a paraphrase records a book or article's main point, but it also recaps the reasons and key evidence supporting that conclusion. Paraphrase any materials you expect to use extensively in a project. Then consider how the research materials you have gathered stand in relationship to each other.

Identify the major claims and the structure of the source.   Determine the main points made by the article, chapter, or text you are paraphrasing, and examine how the work organizes information to support its claims. Then follow the same structure when you paraphrase the source. For example, your paraphrase will probably be arranged sequentially when a work has a story to tell, be arranged topic by topic when you're dealing with reported information, or be structured logically—by claims and evidence—when you take notes from arguments or editorials.

Track the source faithfully.   A paraphrase should move through an article, chapter, or book succinctly while remaining faithful to its purpose, organization, tone, and, to some extent, style. In effect, you are preparing an abstract of the material, complete and readable on its own. Take concise and practical notes, adapting the paraphrase to your needs—understanding that materials especially valuable to your project will need to be described thoroughly.

Record key pieces of evidence.   Thanks to photocopies and downloaded files, you don't usually have to copy data laboriously into your notes—and you probably shouldn't. (Chances of error greatly multiply whenever you transcribe information by hand.) Be certain, though, that your paraphrase sets down supporting reasons for all major claims in the source, as well as key evidence and facts. Key evidence is whatever proves a point or seals the deal in an argument. Keep track of page numbers for all the important data so you can cite this material in your paper without having to return to the original source.

Be certain your notes are entirely in your own words. If you copy the language of sources as you paraphrase them, you risk plagiarism. Deliberately or not, you could transfer big chunks of someone else's writing into your project. But if you have paraphrased by the rules, setting all borrowed words between quotation marks, it's safe to import those notes directly into your project—giving the original writers due credit for their ideas, of course. When you write competent paraphrases, you've already started to compose your own paper. There is no lost motion.

Avoid misleading or inaccurate paraphrasing. **Your notes won't be worth much if your paraphrases of** sources distort the content of what you read. Don't rearrange the information, give it a spin you might prefer, or offer your own opinions on a subject. Make it clear, too, whenever your comments focus just on particular sections or chapters of a source, rather than on the entire piece. That way, you won't misread your notes days later and give readers a wrong impression about an article or book. The following is a paraphrase of "Sanity 101" that gets almost *everything* wrong.

Opening sentences follow language of editorial too closely and also distort structure of editorial. → Parents of teens usually try to be reasonable, the editors of *USA Today* complained on January 19, 2006. But the words "college admission" can make both child and parent irrational. The response is not unreasonable, given all the irritating questions facing parents seeking to improve their children's prospects. But the fact is that just a few colleges are highly selective. Most of the four-year schools in the country have acceptance rates of 85 percent. So

Paraphrase shifts tone, becoming much more colloquial than editorial. → high school students and parents should just chill and not blow their wallets on extra expenses. Rely on the school

Paraphrase borrows words and phrases too freely from original. → admissions counselor; don't hire a private adviser or professional editor to shape your child's college essay. A testing tutor might charge $2,400; a private college counselor can cost from $1,300 to $10,000. This is unfair to poorer families too, especially when companies start offering special admissions services to their employees.

Opinion offered here distorts what is in the editorial. → As always, the colleges are to blame, with their pushy "early admissions" programs, which make them look good in rankings but just screw their students.

Use your paraphrases to synthesize sources. If you are asked to prepare a literature review or synthesis paper on a subject, begin that work by carefully summarizing and paraphrasing a range of reputable sources.

Incorporating Sources into Your Work

When you incorporate sources into your research projects cogently, you give readers information they need to appraise the thinking you've done. They discover what you've read and learned and how much purchase you have on ideas. Yet introducing borrowed ideas and quoted passages into papers is far from easy. You have to help readers identify paraphrased or quoted items, and you need to clearly identify any edits you made to quotations for accuracy or clarity.

Cue the reader in some way whenever you introduce borrowed material. Readers *always* need to know what words and ideas are yours and what you have culled from other authors. So give them a verbal signal whenever you summarize, paraphrase, or quote directly from sources. Think of it as *framing* these borrowed materials to set them off from your own work. Such frames offer many options for introducing either ideas or direct quotes drawn from sources:

Exact Words

> Michelle Obama argued on *The View* that "…[quotation]."

> "[Quotation]…," says Jack Welch, former CEO of General Electric, pointing out that "…[more quotation]."

Summarized Facts

> According to a report in *Scientific American* (October 2012), the Mars rover *Curiosity* will soon…[your own words].

Paraphrased Idea

> Can a person talk intelligently about books even without reading them? Pierre Bayard, for one, suggests that…[your own words].

Your Summary with Quotation

> In *Encounters with the Archdruid*, author John McPhee introduces readers to conservationist David Brower, whom he credits with [your own words], calling him "…[quotation]."

As you see, a frame can introduce, interrupt, follow, or even surround the words or ideas taken from sources, but be sure that your signal phrases are grammatical and lead smoothly into the material.

Select an appropriate "verb of attribution" to frame borrowed material. These "signal verbs" influence what readers think of borrowed ideas or quoted material. Use neutral verbs of attribution in reports; save descriptive or even biased terms for arguments. Note that, by MLA convention, verbs of attribution are usually in the present tense when talking about current work or ideas. (In APA, these verbs are generally in the past or present perfect tense.)

Verbs of Attribution

Neutral	Descriptive	Biased
adds	acknowledges	admits
explains	argues	charges
finds	asserts	confesses
notes	believes	confuses
offers	claims	derides
observes	confirms	disputes
says	disagrees	evades
shows	responds	impugns
states	reveals	pretends
writes	suggests	smears

Use ellipsis marks [...] to shorten a lengthy quotation. When quoting a source in your paper, it's not necessary to use every word or sentence, as long as the cuts you make don't distort the meaning of the original material. An ellipsis mark, formed from three spaced periods, shows where words, phrases, full sentences, or more have been removed from a quotation. The mark doesn't replace punctuation within a sentence. Thus, you might see a period or a comma immediately followed by an ellipsis mark.

Original Passage

Although gift giving has been a pillar of Hopi society, trade has also flourished in Hopi towns since prehistory, <u>with a network that extended from the Great Plains to the Pacific Coast, and from the Great Basin, centered on present-day Nevada and Utah, to the Valley of Mexico.</u> Manufactured goods, raw materials, and gems drove the trade, supplemented by exotic items such as parrots. The Hopis were producers as well, manufacturing large quantities of cotton cloth and ceramics for the trade. To this day, interhousehold trade and barter, especially for items of traditional manufacture for ceremonial use <u>(such as basketry, bows, cloth, moccasins, pottery, and rattles)</u>, remain vigorous.

Underlining shows words to be deleted when passage is quoted.

—Peter M. Whiteley, "Ties That Bind: Hopi Gift Culture and Its First Encounter with the United States," *Natural History*, November 2004, p. 26

Passage with Ellipses

Whiteley has characterized the practice this way:

> Although gift giving has been a pillar of Hopi society, trade has also flourished in Hopi towns since prehistory.... Manufactured goods, raw materials, and gems drove the trade, supplemented by exotic items such as parrots. The Hopis were producers as well, manufacturing large quantities of cotton cloth and ceramics for the trade. To this day, interhousehold trade and barter, especially for items of traditional manufacture for ceremonial use, ...remain vigorous. (26)

Ellipses show where words have been deleted.

Use brackets [ ] to insert explanatory material into a quotation.   By convention, readers understand that the bracketed words are not part of the original material.

> Writing in the *London Review of Books* (January 26, 2006), John Lancaster describes the fears of publishers: "At the moment Google says they have no intention of providing access to this content [scanned books still under copyright]; but why should anybody believe them?"

Use ellipsis marks, brackets, and other devices to make quoted materials fit the grammar of your sentences.   Sometimes, the structure of sentences you want to quote won't quite match the grammar, tense, or perspectives of your own surrounding prose. If necessary, cut up a quoted passage to slip appropriate sections into your own sentences, adding bracketed changes or explanations to smooth the transition.

Original Passage

> Among Chandler's most charming sights are the business-casual dads joining their wives and kids for lunch in the mall food court. The food isn't the point, let alone whether it's from Subway or Dairy Queen. The restaurants merely provide the props and setting for the family time. When those kids grow up, they'll remember the food court as happily as an older generation recalls the diners and motels of Route 66—not because of the businesses' innate appeal but because of the memories they evoke.

Words to be quoted are underlined.

—Virginia Postrel, "In Defense of Chain Stores," *The Atlantic*, December 2006

Material as Quoted

> People who dislike chain stores should ponder the small-town America that cultural critic Virginia Postrel describes, one where "<u>business-casual dads</u> [join] <u>their wives and kids for lunch in the mall food court,</u>" a place that future generations of kids will remember "<u>as happily as an older generation recalls the diners and motels of Route 66.</u>"

Words quoted from source are underlined.

Use [sic] to signal an obvious error in quoted material.   You don't want readers to blame a mistake on you, and yet you are obligated to reproduce a quotation exactly—including blunders in the original. You can highlight an error by putting *sic* (the Latin word for "thus") in brackets immediately following the mistake. The device says, in effect, that this is the way you found it.

> The late Senator Edward Kennedy once took Supreme Court nominee Samuel Alito to task for his record: "In an era when America is still too divided by race and riches, Judge Alioto [sic] has not written one single opinion on the merits in favor of a person of color alleging race discrimination on the job."

Chapter
Nine

Documenting Sources
by John J. Ruszkiewicz and Jay T. Dolmage

Required to document your research paper? It seems simple in theory: List your sources and note where and how you use them. But the practice can be intimidating. For one thing, you have to follow rules for everything from capitalizing titles to captioning images. For another, documentation systems differ between fields. What worked for a Shakespeare paper won't transfer to your psychology research project. Bummer. What do you need to do?

Understand the point of documentation. Documentation systems differ to serve the writers and researchers who use them. Modern Language Association (MLA) documentation, which you probably know from composition and literature classes, highlights author names, books, and article titles and assumes that writers will be quoting a lot—as literature scholars do. American Psychological Association (APA) documentation, gospel in psychology and social sciences, focuses on publication dates because scholars in these fields value the latest research. Council of Science Editors (CSE) documentation, used in the hard sciences, provides predictably detailed advice for handling formulas and numbers.

So systems of documentation aren't arbitrary. Their rules simply reflect the specialized needs of writers in various fields.

Understand what you accomplish through documentation.   First, you clearly identify the sources you have used. In a world awash with information, readers really do need to have reliable information about titles, authors, data, media of publication, and so on.

In addition, by citing your sources, you certify the quality of your research and, in turn, receive credit for your labor. You also provide evidence for your claims. An appreciative reader or instructor can tell a lot from your bibliography alone.

Finally, when you document a paper, you encourage readers to follow up on your work. When you've done a good job, serious readers will want to know more about your subject. Both your citations and your bibliography enable them to take the next step in their research.

Chapter Ten

Annotated Bibliographies

by John J. Ruszkiewicz and Jay T. Dolmage

When you are preparing a term paper, senior thesis, or other lengthy research project, an instructor may expect you to submit an annotated bibliography. The bibliography may be due weeks before you turn in the paper, or it may be turned in with the finished project.

- A sociology instructor asks that your topic proposal for a midterm paper on rural poverty include an annotated bibliography that demonstrates a range of perspectives in your reading.

- Your senior history thesis is based upon letters and archival materials found only in a local museum. So you attach an annotated bibliography to your completed project to give readers a clearer sense of what some of the handwritten documents cover.

- In writing a term paper on the cultural roots and connections of gangsta/reality rap, you decide to annotate your works cited items to let readers know what sources you found most authoritative and useful for future research.

Understanding Annotated Bibliographies

An annotated bibliography is an alphabetical list of the sources and documents you have used in developing a research project, with each item in the list summarized and, very often, evaluated.

Instructors usually ask you to attach an annotated bibliography to the final version of a project so that they can determine at a glance how well you've researched your subject. But some may ask you to submit an annotated bibliography earlier in the writing process—sometimes even as part of the topic proposal—to be sure you're staying on track, poring over good materials, and getting the most out of them.

Begin with an accurate record of research materials. Items recorded in the alphabetical list should follow the guidelines of some documentation system, typically MLA or APA. In a paper using MLA documentation, the list is labeled "Works Cited" and includes only books, articles, and other source materials actually mentioned in the project; it is labeled "Works Consulted" if you also want to include works you've read but not actually cited. In a project using APA style, the list is called "References."

Describe or summarize the content of each item in the bibliography. These summaries should be *very* brief, often just one or two sentences. Begin with a concise description of the work if it isn't self-evident (*a review of; an interview with; a CIA report on*). Then, in your own words, describe its contents, scope, audience, perspective, or other features relevant to your project. Your language should be descriptive and impartial. Be sure to follow any special guidelines offered by your instructor.

Assess the significance or quality of the work. Immediately following the summary, offer a brief appraisal of the item, responding to its authority, thoroughness, length, relevance, usefulness, age (e.g., *up-to-date/dated*), reputation in field (if known), and so on. Your remarks should be professional and academic: You aren't writing a movie review.

Explain the role the work plays in your research. When an annotated bibliography is part of a topic proposal, size up the materials you have found so far and describe how you expect to use them in your project. Highlight the works that provide creative or fresh ideas, authoritative coverage, up-to-date research, diverse perspectives, or ample bibliographies.

Getting the Details Right

You will grasp the value of annotated bibliographies the moment you find a trustworthy one covering a subject you are researching. As you prepare such a list of your own, think how your work might help other readers and researchers.

Record the information on your sources accurately. As you format the items in your list, be sure that the titles, authors, page numbers, and dates are error-free so that users can quickly locate the materials you have used.

Follow a single documentation style. Documentation systems like MLA and APA can seem fussy, but they make life easier for researchers by standardizing the way all the identifying features of a source are treated. So when you get an entry right in your annotated bibliography, you make life easier for the next person who needs to cite that source.

Keep summaries and assessments brief. Don't get carried away. In most cases, instructors and other readers will want an annotated bibliography that they can scan. They'll appreciate writing that is both precise and succinct.

Follow directions carefully. Some instructors may provide specific directions for annotated bibliographies, depending on the field or subject of your research. For example, they may ask you to supply the volume numbers, locations, and physical dimensions of books; describe illustrations; provide URLs; and so on.

Examining a Model

The following three items are from an annotated bibliography offered as part of a topic proposal on the cultural impact of the iPod.

Stephenson, Seth. "You and Your Shadow." *Slate.com*. Slate Group, 2 Mar. 2004. Web. 3 Mar. 2014. This article from *Slate.com*'s "Ad Report Card" series argues that the original iPod ads featuring silhouetted dancers may alienate viewers by suggesting that the product is cooler than the people who buy it. Stephenson explains why some people may resent the advertisements. The piece may be useful for explaining early reactions to the iPod as a cultural phenomenon.

Full bibliographical citation in MLA style.

Summary of Stephenson's argument.

Potential role source might play in paper.

Sullivan, Andrew. "Society Is Dead: We Have Retreated into the iWorld." *Sunday Times*. Times Newspapers, 20 Feb. 2005. Web. 27 Feb. 2014. In this opinion piece, Sullivan examines how people in cities use iPods to isolate themselves from their surroundings. The author makes a highly personal but

Evaluation of Sullivan's opinion piece.

plausible case for turning off the machines. The column demonstrates how quickly the iPod has changed society and culture.

Walker, Rob. "The Guts of a New Machine." *New York Times Magazine*, 30 Nov. 2003. *Academic OneFile*. Web. 1 Mar. 2014. This lengthy report describes in detail how Apple developed the concept and technology of the iPod. Walker not only provides a detailed early look at the product but also shows how badly Apple's competitors underestimated its market strength. May help explain Apple's later dominance in smartphones as well.

Citation demonstrates how to cite an article from a database—in this case, *Academic OneFile*.

Questions to Ask About Your Own Source Use

- Have I chosen "good" sources for this genre?

  o Do my sources meet any specific requirements for the assignment?

  o Are my sources credible in terms of what I'm writing?

  o Are my sources recent enough to be useful and trustworthy for what I'm writing?

  o Have I chosen my sources for my own biased reasons? In other words, am I just choosing sources that agree with me ("confirmation bias")? If the answers to these questions is "yes," then consider your genre and if it requires a better balance or variety of views.

  o How will the reader(s) react to and feel about these sources? Will my sources add to or disrupt my credibility?

- Are my *summaries* well developed?

  o Are they accurate and complete? Do they represent the original author(s) ethically?

  o Do they cover the "big picture" main argument or point of the source?

  o Are they written completely in my own words?

  o Have I used a "verb of attribution" and other framing to introduce each summary?

  o How have I used the summary in my work? Does it have a clear purpose?

- Are my *paraphrases* well developed?

  o Have I chosen the best—most informative and/or more persuasive—section(s) of the source to paraphrase? Does each paraphrase I'm using serve a specific purpose in my project?

  o Do each of my paraphrases represent the author(s) point accurately?

  o Is the paraphrase written completely in my own words?

  o Have I provided a page number (if available) to indicate what part of the source the paraphrase refers to?

  o Have I used a "verb of attribution" and other framing to introduce each paraphrase?

- Are my *quotes* well developed?
    - Have I chosen my quotes carefully? What have been my reasons for choosing to quote versus choosing to paraphrase?
    - If my quote is long, am I sure I need all of it? How can I best use the quote to complement my own writer's voice instead of letting the quote take over?
    - Have I quoted the original source with 100% accuracy?
    - Have I used quotation marks to indicate these are not my own words?
    - Have I provided a source and page number to clarify where the quote came from?
    - Have I used a "verb of attribution" and other framing to introduce each quote?
- Have I followed use of other people's ideas with my own commentary? In other words, have I explained, applied, analyzed, evaluated or in some other way *used* the sources that I've integrated into my project?
- Have I followed the documentation rules (for example, MLA, APA, Chicago, IEEE, etc.) required by this instructor?
- What questions or concerns do I have about my use of sources? When and how can I get answers? For example, is this a good question to ask during class? During an instructor meeting or conference? During a visit to the Writing Center? During peer review?

Questions About Your Own Annotated Bibliographies and Abstracts

Although the reading in this section focuses on Annotated Bibliographies, an abstract of some sort often accompanies this type of assignment. If you have been asked to write only one or the other, then you may want to ignore some of the questions in this list.

- Have I made good choices regarding my sources?
    - ᵒ Have I met the requirements for this assignment/genre?
    - ᵒ Do I have the number of sources that the instructor requires or expects?
    - ᵒ Do I have the *types* of sources (peer-reviewed/scholarly, trade, popular, personal) sources my instructor expects and/or that this genre requires?
- Are my bibliographic records accurate?
- Have I followed the documentation rules (for example, MLA, APA, Chicago, IEEE, etc.) required by this instructor?
- Are my sources in alphabetical order?
- Are my annotations thorough?
    - ᵒ Does each annotation include a brief summary of the source?
    - ᵒ Does each annotation comment on the quality of the source?
    - ᵒ Does each annotation indicate what about the source is useful to me and my project?
- Does each annotation meet my instructor's specific requirements, such as length minimums or maximums? Are they written in the tone (most often formal, scholarly) that my instructor expects?
- Does my abstract meet the requirements set forth by my instructor: length, style, emphasis?
- Does my abstract help make sense of my annotated bibliography, and does my annotated bibliography lead to better understanding of my abstract? In other words, do the two work together as a whole?

Section Five

Peer Reviewing and Preparing to Submit Your Work

Some students (and even some instructors!) struggle with peer review because it can seem unproductive or even confusing. That said, peer review is also very important. It provides different perspectives on the clarity and content of your work and gives you a chance to see how other people have approached the same writing tasks. Having your work read by others who know about the genre and expectations for the project can make your writing much stronger—that's why the "scholarly" writing done by professors and researchers undergoes rather strict peer review before it's published. The most important aspect of peer review is the attitude with which everyone—students and instructors—approach it. "The Writer's Workshop: Making the Most of Peer Review" is included to help break down the purposes and approaches to peer review as well as to suggest strategies for making it most helpful. Remember, peer review is an indispensable part of revision—which is key to the writing process.

Chapter Eleven

The Writer's Workshop
by Bruce P. Ballenger

Making the Most of Peer Review

Sharing your writing with strangers can be among the most frightening and gratifying social experiences. It can be a key to the success of the next draft or a complete waste of time. One thing sharing your writing can't be, however, is avoided, at least in most composition courses, which these days frequently rely on small and large group workshops to help students revise. This is a good thing, I think, for three reasons:

1. It's useful to experience *being read* by others.

2. Workshops can be among the most effective ways for writers to divorce the draft.

3. The talk about writing in workshops can be enormously instructive.

Being Read

Being read is not the same thing as being read to. As we share our writing, sometimes reading our own work aloud to a group, we are sharing ourselves in a very real way. This is most evident with a personal essay, but virtually any piece of writing bears our authorship—our particular ways of seeing and saying things—and included in this are our feelings about ourselves as writers.

Last semester, Matthew told me that he felt he was the worst writer in the class, and that seemed obvious when I watched him share his writing in his workshop group. Matthew was quiet and compliant, readily accepting suggestions with little comment, and he seemed to rush the conversation about his draft as if to make the ordeal end sooner. When Matthew's drafts were discussed, his group always ended in record time, and yet he always claimed that they were "helpful."

Tracy always began presenting her drafts by announcing, "This really sucks. It's the worst thing I've ever written." Of course it wasn't. But this announcement seemed intended to lower the stakes for her, to take some of the pressure off of her performance in front of others, or, quite possibly, it was a hopeful invitation for Tracy's group members to say, "You're too hard on yourself. This is really good."

To *be read* in a workshop group can mean more than a critique of your ideas or sentences; for students like Matthew and Tracy it is an evaluation of *themselves*, particularly their self-worth as writers. Of course, this isn't the purpose of peer review at all, but for those of us with sometimes nagging internal critics, it's pretty hard to avoid feeling that both your writing and your writing self are on trial. This is why it's so helpful to articulate these fears before being read. It's also helpful to imagine the many positive outcomes that might come from the experience of sharing your writing.

While taking workshop comments about your writing personally is always a risk, consider the really rare and unusual opportunity to *see* readers respond to your work. I often compare my published writing to dropping a very heavy stone down a deep well and waiting to hear the splash. And waiting. And waiting. But in a workshop, you can actually hear the murmurs, the sighs, and the laughter of your readers as you read to them; you can also see the smiles, puzzled expressions, nodding heads, and even tears. You can experience your readers' experiences of your writing in ways that most published authors never can.

What is so valuable about this, I think, is that audience is no longer an abstraction. After your first workshop, it's no stretch to imagine the transaction that most writing involves—a writer's words being received by a reader who thinks and feels something in response. And when you take this back to the many solitary hours of writing, you may feel you have company; that members of your workshop group are interested in what you have to say.

This is a powerful thing. In some ways, it's the most important thing about the workshop experience.

Divorcing the Draft

Our writing relationships include our emotional connection to drafts, and this often has to do with the time we spent writing them. Sometimes we need to divorce a draft, and the best remedy for this is time away from it. But students rarely have that luxury.

Workshops provide an alternative to time away from a draft and are effective for the same reason some people see therapists—group members offer an "outsider's" perspective on your work that may give it new meanings and raise new possibilities. If nothing else, readers offer a preview of whether your current meanings are clear and whether what you assume is apparent *is* apparent to someone other than yourself. It's rare when a workshop doesn't jerk writers away from at least a few of their assumptions about a draft, and the best of these experiences inspire writers to want to write again. This is the outcome we should always hope to attain.

Instructive Talk

Consider a few comments I overheard during workshops recently:

- "I don't think the focus is clear in this essay. In fact, I think there are at least two separate essays here, and it's the one on the futility of antiwar protests I'm most interested in."

- "Do you think that there's a better lead buried on the third page, in the paragraph about your sister's decision to go to the hospital? That was a powerful scene, and it seemed to be important to the overall theme."

- "I was wondering about something. What is it about the idea that we sometimes keep silent not only to protect other people but to protect ourselves that surprised you? I mean, does knowing that change anything about how you feel about yourself as a parent?"

- "I loved this line. Simply loved it."

The talk in workshops is not always about writing. The "underlife" of the classroom often surfaces in workshops, a term one educator uses to describe the idle talk about the class itself. Most writing classes ask students to step out of their usual student roles. Rather than quietly listen to lectures or study a textbook, in a writing course you are asked to make your own meanings and find your own ways of making meaning. Whenever we are asked to assume new roles, some resistance can set in, and workshops can become an occasion for talk about the class, often out of earshot of the instructor. This talk isn't always complaining. Often workshops are opportunities to share understandings or approaches to assignments and especially experiences with them. They can also be a chance for students to try out new identities—"I really liked writing this. Maybe I'm an okay writer after all."

While this kind of talk may not be directly about a draft, it can help you negotiate the new roles you're being asked to assume in your writing class. This is part of becoming better writers who are confident that they can manage the writing process in all kinds of situations. However, the main purpose of workshop groups is to help students revise their drafts. But why seek advice from writers who are clearly less experienced than the instructor?

1. By talking with other students about writing, you get practice using the language you're learning in the writing classroom, language that helps you describe important features of your own work.

2. Because writing is about making choices among a range of solutions to problems in a draft, workshop groups are likely to surface possibilities that never occurred to you (and perhaps wouldn't occur to the instructor, either).

3. Your peers are also student writers and because they come from similar circumstances—demands of other classes, part-time jobs, and perhaps minimal experience with college writing—they are in a position to offer practical and realistic revision suggestions.

4. Finally, in most writing courses, the students in the class are an important audience for your work. Getting firsthand responses makes the rhetorical situation real rather than imagined.

Will you get bad advice in a peer workshop? Of course. Your group members will vary in their experience and ability to read the problems and possibilities in a draft. But in the best writing workshops, you learn together, and as time goes by the feedback gets better and better. Paradoxically, it pays off in your own writing to be generous in your responses to the work of others.

The Writer's Responsibilities

No matter what model your instructor chooses, the success of the workshop depends largely on the writers themselves. Sure, it can be harder to get what you need from some groups, but in the end, you can always get *some* help with a draft if you ask the right questions and seek certain kinds of responses.

How should you prepare for a workshop to make the most of it, and what are your responsibilities during the workshop? Here's a list you might find helpful:

• Make sure everyone in the group gets a copy of the draft in a timely way.

• Reread and reflect on the draft before the workshop session. What kinds of responses would be most helpful from your group? What questions do you have about the draft's possible problems?

- Time the discussion so that your draft gets the allotted time and no more, particularly if there are other drafts to discuss.

- Avoid getting defensive. Listen to comments on your work in an open-minded way. Your obligation is simply to listen, not to take all the advice you're offered.

- Take notes. There are two reasons for this. First, it will help you remember other students' comments and, second, it will signal that you take those comments seriously. This increases everyone's engagement with your work.

The Reader's Responsibilities

Tina poured her heart and soul into her personal essay draft, and she was eager to get some response to it. When it was her turn to workshop the piece, however, one of the group's members was absent, and two others failed to write her the required response. "It was so lame," she told me. "It was as if no one cared about my essay. It sure makes me feel less inclined to read their stuff carefully." If this workshop group were at Hewlett-Packard or any of the thousands of businesses that encourage teamwork, the slackers would be in trouble. But teamwork in the writing class depends more on internal motivation—a sense of responsibility to others—than any external reward or punishment. There is some external motivation: It pays to be generous with your responses to others' work because you'll learn more about your own.

You can increase your own learning in a workshop and contribute to a writer's positive experience by taking the following responsibilities seriously:

- Always read and respond to a writer's draft in a timely way. The writer may suggest the type of response that would be most helpful; if so, always keep that in mind.

- Whenever possible, focus your responses on particular parts or passages of the draft but, except in an editorial workshop, avoid a focus on grammar or mechanics.

- Offer suggestions, not directives. The word *could* is usually better than *should*. Remember that the purpose of the workshop is to help identify the range of choices a writer might make to improve a draft. There is almost always more than one.

- Identify strengths in the draft. This is often a good place to begin because it sets writers at ease, but, more important, writers often build on strengths in revision.

- Consider varying the roles you play in conversation with your group (see the "Inquiring into the Details: Finding a Role" box). It's easy to fall into a rut in group work, pretty much sticking to saying the same kinds of things or developing certain patterns of response. Stay vigilant about this and try deliberately shifting the role you play in the workshop group.

Inquiring into the Details

Finding a Role

"Slacker" is a role that's easy to slide into in small-group work. It's completely passive, and it's really pretty selfish. Active roles ask more of you, but they pay off big because you learn more about your own writing. You might assume any of several active roles in a writing workshop group. Try them out.

Roles That Help Groups Get Things Done

Initiators: "Here's how we might proceed with this."

Information seekers: "What do we need to know to help the writer?"

Information givers: "This seems to be an important example."

Opinion seekers: "What do you think, Al?"

Opinion givers: "I think this works."

Clarifiers: "We all seem to be saying that the lead doesn't deliver, right?"

Elaborators: "I agree with Tom, and would add…"

Summarizers: "I think we've discussed the thesis problem enough. Should we move on to the evidence?"

Roles That Help Maintain Group Harmony

Encouragers: "I love that idea, Jen."

Expressivists: "My silence isn't because I 'm not moved by the essay, but I'm still trying to figure out why. Is that why you're quiet, Leah?"

Harmonizers: "I think we disagree about this, but that's okay. Let's move on to discussing this next page."

Compromisers: "Maybe both Richard and Joseph are right, particularly if we look at it this way…"

Gatekeepers: "Jon, we haven't heard anything from you yet."

What Can Go Wrong and What to Do About It

Lana is not a fan of workshops. In an argument essay, she complained that they "lack quality feedback," and sometimes workshop groups encourage "fault finding" that can hurt the writer and the writing. Things can go wrong in workshops, of course, and when they do students like Lana feel burned. Typically, unsuccessful workshop groups suffer from two major problems: lack of commitment by group members and lack of clarity about the process of giving feedback. It's like a cold and a runny nose—when a group is afflicted with one problem it usually suffers from the other.

Lack of commitment is easy to see. The writer whose draft is to be discussed forgets to make copies for the rest of her group. Members who were supposed to provide written responses to a writer's draft before class hastily make notes on his manuscript as it's being discussed. The group is supposed to allot fifteen minutes to discuss each draft but finishes in five. Members are frequently absent and make no effort to provide responses to drafts they missed. Discussion is limited to general, not particularly thoughtful, compliments: "This is really good. I wouldn't change a thing," or "Just add a few details."

This lack of commitment is contagious and soon infects nearly every group meeting. Things rarely improve; they frequently get worse. Part of the problem may be that workshop participants are not clear on what is expected of them, a problem that should be minimized if you reviewed the checklists about the writer's and reader's responsibilities in workshop, discussed in the preceding sections. A solution that is beyond your control is that the instructor evaluates or even grades workshop participation, but a group can evaluate itself, too. Questions members should ask when evaluating their group can include: How effectively does your group work together? How would you evaluate the participation of group members? How do you feel about your own performance? How satisfied were you with the responses to your draft?

Groups that work together over a period of time should always monitor how things are going, and the group evaluations can be particularly helpful for this. If problems persist, the instructor may intervene or the group might consider intervention of its own. Remember, the best workshops have a simple but powerful effect on writers who share their work: *It makes them want to write again.*

Questions to Ask Yourself About Peer Feedback

Pre-Peer Review

- Do I understand the purpose of peer review (especially the difference between reviewing for content and structure versus copyediting)?

- Do I understand how our English 1010 peer reviews contribute to the writing process?

- Do I understand the value of an outsider's viewpoint on my draft(s)?

- Do I know how to comment most effectively?

- Do I understand the value of taking time away from my draft in order to see it more objectively?

- How will I be a responsible, considerate, and reflective peer reviewer?

  - Monitor my time with peer essays.

  - Make suggestions on specific passages.

  - Give positive feedback where appropriate.

  - Commit to being a part of the writing process.

- What would I like to receive feedback on?

  - My thesis or argument structure?

  - My sources, in-text citations, and/or documentation?

  - My paragraph structure (topic sentences, evidence, analysis/application)?

  - My overall focus?

  - The tone, precision, and "artfulness" of my language?

  - My introduction and/or conclusion?

  - Something else?

- What do I hope to gain from getting my work reviewed by my peers? How can I be the mostly helpful when, in turn, reviewing their work?

Post-Peer Review

- In what ways did I benefit from peer review?

- Was I prepared with the required materials (such as printed drafts)?

- Did I ask for specific feedback on my draft? If so, did I get what I hoped for in terms of review and/or advice?

- Did my peers and I manage our peer review time effectively?

- Was I open to all my peers' feedback?
- Did I take notes on, or otherwise document, my peers' feedback?
- Have I asked follow-up questions when I wanted to better understand my peers' advice?
- Have I considered what peer feedback I would like to implement?
- Have I made a plan for revising?
- Would a Writing Center visit be useful?
- Do I need to talk to my instructor about anything?

Questions as You Prepare to Submit Your Work

- Have I made all the revisions I want to make?

    o   Have I carefully considered the assignment instructions and requirements, to make sure that I met them all?

    o   Have I incorporated formative advice and feedback from my instructor?

    o   Have I incorporated good advice from my peer reviews?

    o   Have I looked back over my class notes and materials—especially any assignment checklists—to make sure that I'm demonstrating the skills my instructor is looking for?

- What do I think are the strengths of my draft? Where would I like to spend more time working on it?

- Do I want any specific feedback from my instructor when this is reviewed?

- What are the specific requirements for when and how my instructor or other audiences want me to submit my work?

    o   What is the specific date/time deadline? What happens if I miss that deadline?

    o   Is the submission on paper? If so, do I know how I'll make a printout?

    o   Is the submission via email or online (such as WyoCourses)? If so, then do I know what types of files are accepted? For example, am I limited to DOCX or PDF? Do I know how to "Save as…" or convert to those file types if needed?